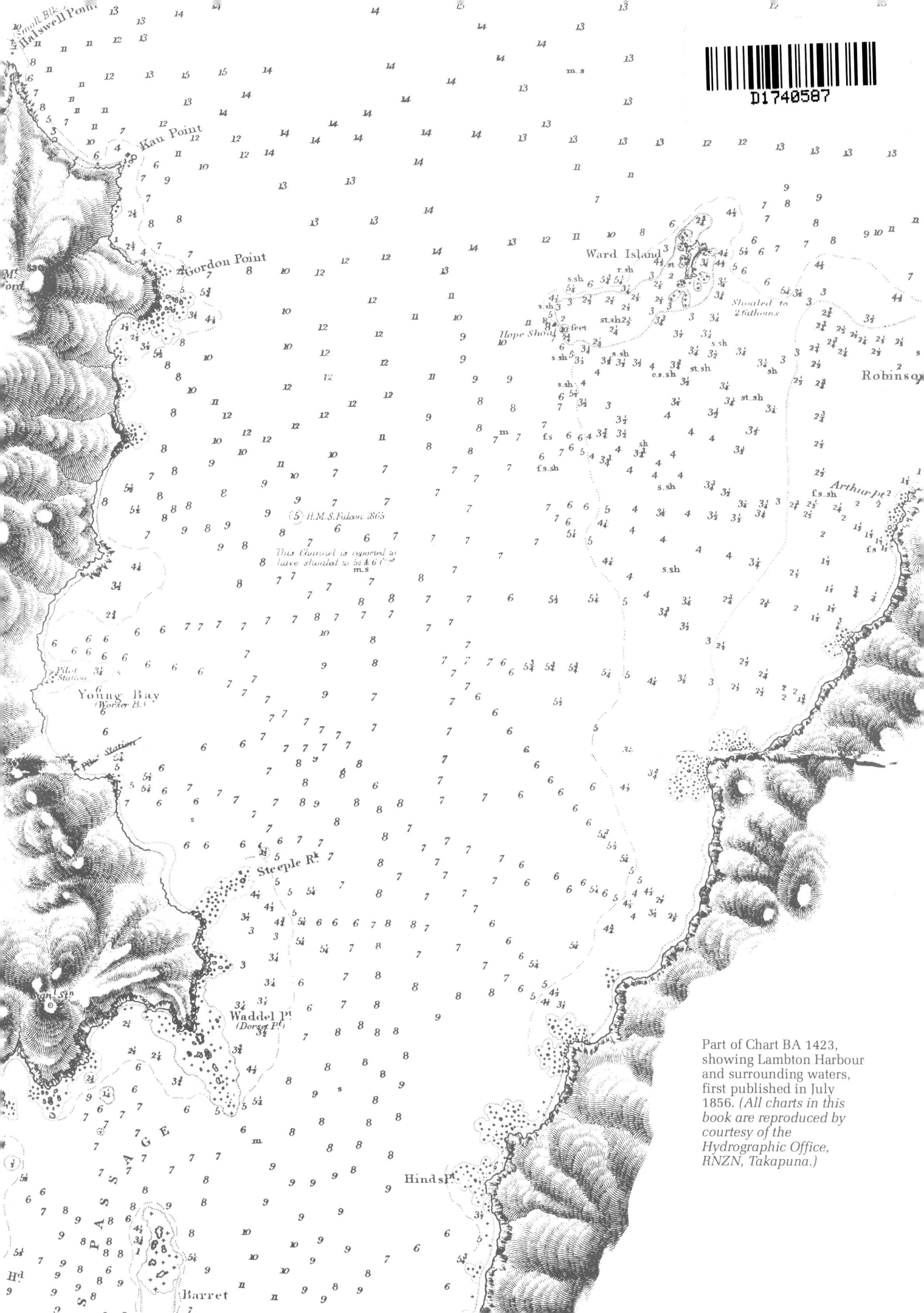

Part of Chart BA 1423, showing Lambton Harbour and surrounding waters, first published in July 1856. *(All charts in this book are reproduced by courtesy of the Hydrographic Office, RNZN, Takapuna.)*

Wellington by the Sea

WELLINGTON BY THE SEA

100 Years of Work and Play

David Johnson

David Bateman

First published in 1990
by David Bateman Ltd
'Golden Heights', 32-34 View Road, Glenfield,
Auckland, New Zealand

ISBN 1-86953-040-3

Typeset in 9½/10 Melior by Bryan Coppersmith,
Auckland
Printed by Colorcraft
Jacket design by Chris O'Brien

Contents

Introduction

Wellington, Harbour Capital the slogans say, and a good description it is. Windy Wellington say others, and that fits too.

Tara and his people moved south from what is now Hawkes Bay to settle in Wellington because of its harbour, Te Whanganui a Tara, the Great Harbour of Tara. Centuries later pakeha settlers also chose Wellington because of its harbour, and the town has since gone about its business in an atmosphere made bracing by the salty tang in the air.

Port Nicholson, as it was named in the 1820s, is a jewel of a harbour. On a fine day it sparkles with an intensity that emphasises the contrast of its still waters with the unpredictability of Cook Strait, just outside. It epitomises the role of a harbour as a haven, a place of shelter.

Wellington settlement grew to become a town, and later the capital city. It has extended beyond its initial setting, spread up the valley of the Hutt River, clutched precariously at the shores facing the wild strait, and moved northwards along the west coast to enfold the harbours and bays there. For years the coast facing Kapiti was a place of sandhills and weekend baches. Much of it is now commuter country.

Yet Wellington retains its essential character of a harbour settlement on the shores of a haven safe from the world outside. That it became the capital city is an accident of geography. It was centrally situated, and in the days when those who governed came by sailing ship and later by steamer, location was all important.

Today, with much of Wellington's post-war industrial growth slowed and many of its major commercial concerns having moved north, its governmental role has become much more dominant, the city more Canberra-like.

This book does not concern itself with politics, industrial expansion at the Hutt, or the replacement of much of downtown Wellington by tall concrete monuments to insurance, finance and diplomacy, but with what the town and its people looked like in the first hundred years after the arrival of the pakeha.

The majority of the illustrations came from the magnificent collection of the Alexander Turnbull Library, where Joan McCracken and her staff were always keen to help. The collection of the Wellington Harbour Board Maritime Museum, from which Emmanuel Makarios readily produced many albums, is a comprehensive record of the development of the port. To complete the selection there are a few illustrations from the files of the Auckland Public Library.

David Johnson
May 1990

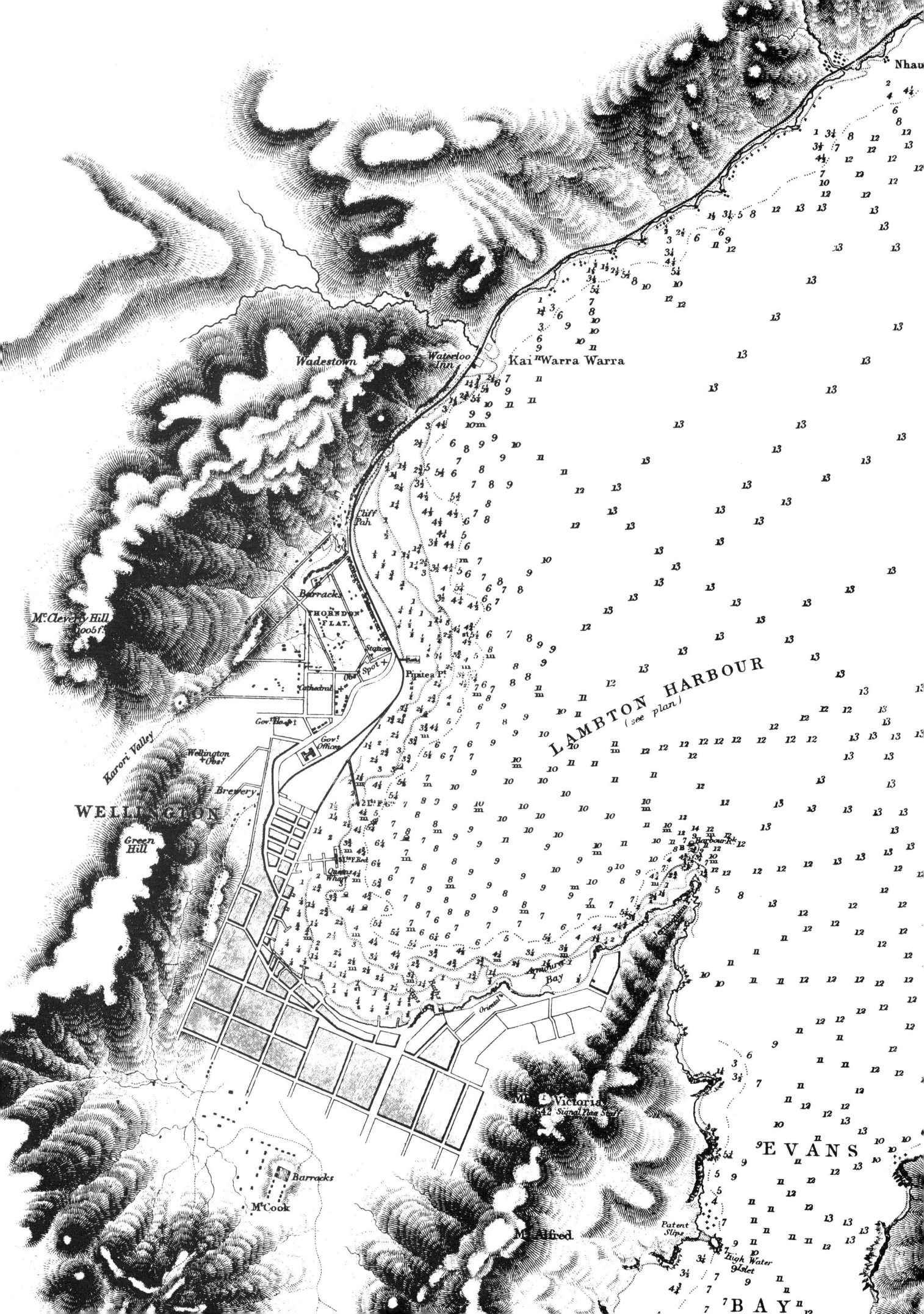

1. The First Half Century

Wellington grows, 1840-1890

In September 1839 Colonel William Wakefield bought most of the land around Wellington harbour from representatives of the Maori people who lived in the area. He paid in the customary currency of the time: muskets, tomahawks, red blankets and a miscellany of trade goods. Wakefield acted for the New Zealand Company, whose first settlers arrived soon after the purchase.

It was a brave settlement: a frontier town established in what was generally regarded as an unhospitable country. New Zealand was not then a colony of Great Britain; Wakefield's purchase preceded the treaty of Waitangi.

The first settlers landed on the shingly beach between the Hutt River and the sea. There, at Petone, a tent settlement sprang up while the New Zealand Company's surveyors got on with the job of sorting out a plan for the town on the other side of the harbour. Petone had flat land, farming potential, and was wide open to the southerly gales that not too infrequently rolled in from Cook Strait. The other side had less flat land, though there was a limited area at Thorndon and at Te Aro, but it had shelter and a better aspect.

To get from Petone to Lambton Harbour, as the other side was called, it was necessary to go by boat or to clamber around the rocks. Boats left regularly from the many pubs which doubled as meeting houses and passenger and freight depots. The boats were small and often overloaded, the weather unpredictable, and accidents frequent.

The creation of a road around the harbour edge was a matter of some priority. To hack a route capable of accommodating a coach or cart required enormous effort, and for some years the road was a mixture of cleared seashore, where boulders had been rolled out of the way, and the occasional cut. It was a low-tide road, but it was a road.

Henry Melville's steel engraving, based on a drawing by S.C. Brees, depicts a horsedrawn cart beginning its journey from Petone, with Wellington in the distance.
Alexander Turnbull Library

Lambton Harbour and Evans Bay, from Chart BA 1423 (1856).

G. Palmer

Incons

Acheron

Lieutenant General T.B. Collinson was, like most senior military men, able to take his pencil and sketch pad to high ground and record the scene before him. When he made this sketch late in 1849 the ship *Inconstant* had, true to her name, missed stays and run ashore near Pencarrow Heads. She was refloated with the assistance of HMS *Acheron*, seen here on the far left. The *Acheron* was engaged in surveying much of New Zealand's coastline. The *Inconstant* was beached at Te Aro, where she can be seen here over the top of the large house in the foreground originally built for Colonel Wakefield.

The town of Wellington straggles along the foreshore in a thin line, with new houses following the roads up the more accessible valleys. Barracks are perched on Mount Cook. The Te Aro pa is on the foreshore to the left of Mount Cook.
Alexander Turnbull Library

This view of the Thorndon Flat end of town "taken from J.P.'s land" was sketched by John Pearse in the mid-1850s from Wellington Terrace, now named simply The Terrace. At the end of Clay Point in the sketch of the Lambton Quay end of town is Plimmer's Wharf, better known as Noah's Ark. Plimmer bought the hulk of the *Inconstant* in 1850 for 50 pounds and had it removed to Clay Point in front of Barrett's Hotel. There the hulk became both a warehouse and a wharf, connected to the shore by a bridge. The building constructed on the deck was occupied by James Smith & Co who celebrated the opening of their auction rooms in May 1851. *Alexander Turnbull Library*

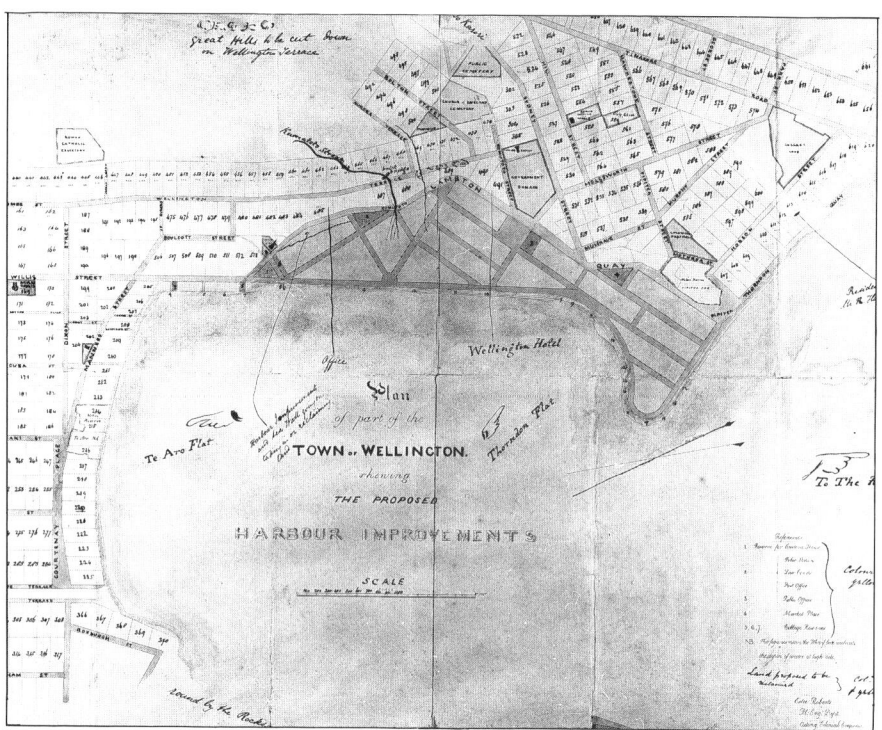

T.S. Ralph's plan "shewing the Proposed Harbour Improvements" notes that "great hills" are to be cut down from Wellington Terrace. The narrow line of surveyed lots between Wellington Terrace and Lambton Quay accentuates the steepness of the cliff behind the foreshore and gives point to Pearse's description of a "difficult and dangerous clamber or crawl" in the notes on his sketch.

Where Lambton Quay meets Boulcott Street an irregular line indicates where spoil has been pushed onto the foreshore and retained by a wall — the first harbour reclamation. The brick bridge over the Kumitoto Stream was a major boon; after a storm the stream was apt to sweep down the cliff, dividing Wellington Terrace and Lambton Quay into two separate sections.

The Te Aro pa site is at the foot of Taranaki Street. While the cutting down of the "great hills" and the recovery of land from the sea were being considered, development of the town was concentrated on the Te Aro flat and the gentler slopes behind Thorndon.
Alexander Turnbull Library

Clay Point. Smith's auction flag flies from Noah's Ark and a coastal schooner is berthed alongside the *Inconstant*, now Plimmer's Wharf. The earthquake of 1855 threw the *Inconstant* on her side but John Plimmer righted her, repaired her, and shored up his investment with a retaining wall.

Across the road is Holdsworth, Knowles & Co's store, the second Barrett's Hotel (the first was further along the quay towards Thorndon) and the imposing frontage of the Atheneum.
Alexander Turnbull Library
(engraving by W.H. Holmes)

Te Aro flat, 1857. Manners Street peters out into a track glorified on the maps as Courtenay Place. Kent Terrace runs off to the right at the rear, overlooked by neatly fenced farmlets on the slope of the hill.

Rhodes' wharf extends out across the beach from Rhodes & Co's warehouse to water deep enough to accommodate small sailing vessels. W.B. Rhodes, proprietor of the firm, was a former seafarer and traded with the whalers at Kapiti. He became a member of Parliament and a director of a number of public companies. His wharf was probably the first that looked like a permanent structure. The square-looking building in the centre is Kebbell's mill, and to the right, on Manners Street, is the Wesleyan Chapel.
Alexander Turnbull Library

Te Aro in 1858 had a grandstand view of a harbour cluttered with round-hulled, square-rigged vessels from the Old Country, barques and brigs from across the Tasman, and little schooners and cutters engaged in the coastal trade.
*Alexander Turnbull Library
(Richard Taylor)*

△ By 1860 reclamation was under
way as men with picks and shovels
hacked into the cliff between
Lambton Quay and Wellington
Terrace and tipped the spoil into
the sea. Clay Point disappeared.
The *Inconstant* was partially
buried and built over. Barrett's
Hotel is the dark coloured building
second from right. Holdsworth
Knowles' store shown in Holmes'
engraving is obscured by the large
new store on the site of Noah's
Ark. On the ledge above Barrett's
Hotel is John Plimmer's workshop.
Willis Street is at centre left,
behind the man with the spade.
Along from Barrett's Hotel is the
Atheneum, one of Wellington's few
public halls, with its mock-stone
wooden facade. Next to it is the
Presbyterian church. A great chunk
of the cliff behind Lambton Quay
has crossed the road to extend the
land into the sea.
Alexander Turnbull Library

▽ Beyond the great excavation runs a long line of shops and pubs. The Crown and Anchor faces the flagstaff and the sea. The small store two buildings to the right is E.W. Mills' ironmongery store. His foundry was in Wellington Terrace. One of the first buildings on the reclamation was the Oddfellows' Hall, its size accentuated by the row of stores in Lambton Quay. Beneath the seawall fronting Lambton Quay was a muddy beach which received clay and filth from stormwater drains and sewers. The sweep of Lambton Quay continues with the South Seas Hotel to the right of centre. In the centre is Mills' Lion Foundry in Wellington Terrace. Towards the left the crumbling edge of Lambton Quay has been shored up with barrels filled with rocks.
Alexander Turnbull Library

As W. Tonks and his men filled in the foreshore with spoil hauled along Lambton Quay by horsedrawn trolleys on a tramway, Queens Wharf, Wellington's first public wharf, was built. A public warehouse and bond store built at its head was named the Queen's Bond, and this name spread to the wharf.
Alexander Turnbull Library (Wilkinson collection)

Queen's Bond at left, Queens Wharf beyond it. On the private wharf in the foreground a hand trolley was used to get goods to and from coastal vessels such as the schooner moored across the end of the wharf. For particularly difficult loads a horse might be called in to help with the trolley. To the left are watermen's boats. The watermen were the harbour's messengers, ferrying crewmen to their vessels at anchor, taking ship's agents about their business, carrying parcels or workers, and sometimes going fishing. Wellington's fishermen often cleaned their fish at the harbour edge of Lambton Quay, adding their contribution to the mess below the seawall.
Wellington Maritime Museum

Queens Wharf in 1867. Left of centre, obscuring the small private jetty, is the headquarters of the New Zealand Steam Navigation Co Ltd. The NZSN Co had grown from a local partnership to become the largest shipping line in the colony, but despite its large fleet and substantial share capital the company had already reached the end of its reign when its new office was constructed. It made a loss in 1866, illustrating the inability of coal-eating steamers to compete with cheaper and slower sailing ships unless there were government subsidies, mail contracts, or very high passenger fares. After another decade of bickering and a capital reconstruction the NZSN Co died with barely a whimper.
Wellington Maritime Museum

At Te Aro more stores and warehouses were built and housing spread over the flat. In 1870 private wharves were still busy although steamers and large sailing vessels patronised Queens Wharf, run by the Provincial Government. Towards the left is Kebbell's mill (with the high roof). In the centre, on the far side of Manners Street, is the Wesleyan Chapel.

Te Aro became Wellington's main shipwrighting and boatbuilding centre. Two slipways are tucked into the corner to the right of centre.
Wellington Maritime Museum

Newspaper editors became increasingly fond of claiming that steam would rule the waves and New Zealand and the Old Country would become closer as a result. Proof of this came in January 1870 when a Royal Navy Flying Squadron visited port. Although the vessels looked very much like the traditional wooden walls of Nelson's days, the four largest ships were screw frigates.

The visit of Admiral Hornby and his men was cause for great jubilation. The Squadron was greeted by bunting-bedecked steamers loaded with well-wishers. There was a public ball at Government Buildings in honour of Hornby and his officers (gentlemen's tickets one pound ten shillings, ladies' ten shillings). A "Grand Dejeuner" was held at Mr Laing's picnic grounds at the Hutt, and the steamer *St Kilda* was laid on by the Government to run from Queens Wharf to Petone.

Caledonian Sports were held at the Cricket Ground where the sailors joined in with enthusiasm, participating in "dancing, kiss-in-the-ring, and a variety of other amusements and sports not in the programme or under the direction of the committee".

And there were speeches. Long, patriotic speeches. The Navy was described as the right arm of the British Empire and its journey to far-flung colonies such as New Zealand compared with the way in which the milky way encircled the heavens. With the Navy's might at anchor in Port Nicholson, Wellingtonians felt safe.
Auckland Public Library

Rosario,   Barossa,   Endym

FLYING SQUADRO

By 1871 the principal reclamation area was complete, streets had been created and many buildings constructed. Here, ships at Queens Wharf are dressed in honour of a public holiday. Captain Daniel McIntyre, the United States consul, flies the stars and stripes from McIntyre & Co's shipchandlery on the reclamation, left.
Alexander Turnbull Library

scylla,   Liverpool, Flag ship.   Phœbe,   Liffey. .

· Rear·Admiral Hornby   Wellington   January 25ᵗʰ 1870. ———

As reclamation left Lambton Quay further from the foreshore, the new Customhouse Quay was formed. At right is the Queen's Bond and beyond it the entrance to Queens Wharf. To the left is the Bank of Australasia with the Inspector's Department adjoining at the far left. The upstairs windows boast venetian blinds. Further along the street, outside the pub, is a gas lamp. The dray is carrying barrels.
Alexander Turnbull Library

By 1880 Te Aro was the industrial centre. Slipways extend down the tongue of mud and sand. Foundries and a multitude of small businesses associated with shipping crowd the area between Courtenay Place and the sea. To the right of centre is the gasometer.
Alexander Turnbull Library

Government House, sited where the Beehive stands today, commanded a view across shops and offices to the harbour. Behind is St Mary's Cathedral and to the right Parliament Buildings, now the General Assembly Library. Bowen Street runs from bottom right behind the shops, which are at the end of Lambton Quay.

The shop with three square-framed windows upstairs has a window display of bottles. The small building in the centre is occupied by H.T. Price, hairdresser and tobacconist. On the right is Mrs Hill's Registry office above the shop of a manufacturing jeweller. Mrs Hill's entrance is probably through the door at the extreme right of the picture. Through this door would pass young ladies in search of employment as maids in the homes of Wellington's leading families.
Auckland Public Library

In 1880 a Harbour Board was formed. Queens Wharf was owned by the Wellington City Council which had inherited it after the abolition of the Provincial Government in 1876. The Council was not keen to hand over a good source of revenue and the Harbour Board began with only the newly constructed Railway Wharf seen here. Queens Wharf is in the background, right.

The old sailing vessel *Jubilee* is berthed at the left. She was bought by the Gear Meat Company after the successful development of the frozen meat trade from 1881 and converted into a floating storeship. She was moored at the end of a wharf in front of Gear's premises until her cargo of frozen carcases was required for a shipment to England. A steamer was then hired to push her across the harbour.
Alexander Turnbull Library (William Williams)

By 1883 the reclamation of the Te Aro foreshore was beginning. The seawall has cut off the slipways near the gasometer but a gap can be seen at the left, providing access to the slipway. There are new boatsheds and slipways where the cliff has been cut back for the road to Oriental Bay. In the foreground are the tops of buildings in Willis Street, including the Christchurch Boarding House. A sign on a small building below the steamer on the slipway proclaims "Dentist" while another sign immediately below it advertises horse and cattle medicines. In the centre A. Rickman proclaims himself to be an Importer & Manufacturer of First Class Boots & Shoes.
Alexander Turnbull Library (William Williams)

One of Te Aro's principal industries was foundrywork and boilermaking.
Luke & Co's foundry and engineering works occupied an acre and a half.
The firm employed 90 workers, and up to 130 in a busy year. They built
anything and everything that used iron or copper, including cranes for the
Harbour Board, ships and engines for ships, dairying utensils, boilers,
and even coal ranges. At a time when excelling was something to be
proud of and "IXL" was a popular brand Lukes went one better; their coal
ranges bore the letters "WEXL" along with a representation of a leg of
mutton.
Alexander Turnbull Library

On the foreshore near Queens
Wharf, on the site of the old
telegraph office, a magnificent new
post office was built, but was
destroyed by fire in 1885. It was
rebuilt, but with a different tower.
This is the building which was
burnt. In front of its main door is a
lifeboat on davits, available for use
in emergencies. Drownings in the
vicinity of Queens Wharf were not
uncommon, especially when
seamen returning from nearby
pubs late at night tried to jump
from wharf to ship or from one
ship to another moored alongside.
Wellington Maritime Museum

In 1885, when buildings that had been constructed on the new ground at
Thorndon shortly after it was reclaimed were being torn down for a new
generation of brick buildings, the remains of Plimmer's Ark, the good ship
Inconstant, were uncovered. The Bank of New Zealand was built on this site.
Alexander Turnbull Library

Most of the development
continued to be concentrated on
the newly reclaimed areas and Te
Aro through the 1880s. There was
building on the hills behind
Thorndon, but the foreshore at that
end of town remained relatively
untouched.

At Pipitea Point children muck
about on the foreshore where
dinghies, an old hull, seaweed and
the flotsam and jetsam of a harbour
provide plenty of interest. Pipitea
Point was the gathering point for
the first serious Wellington
yachties.
Wellington Maritime Museum

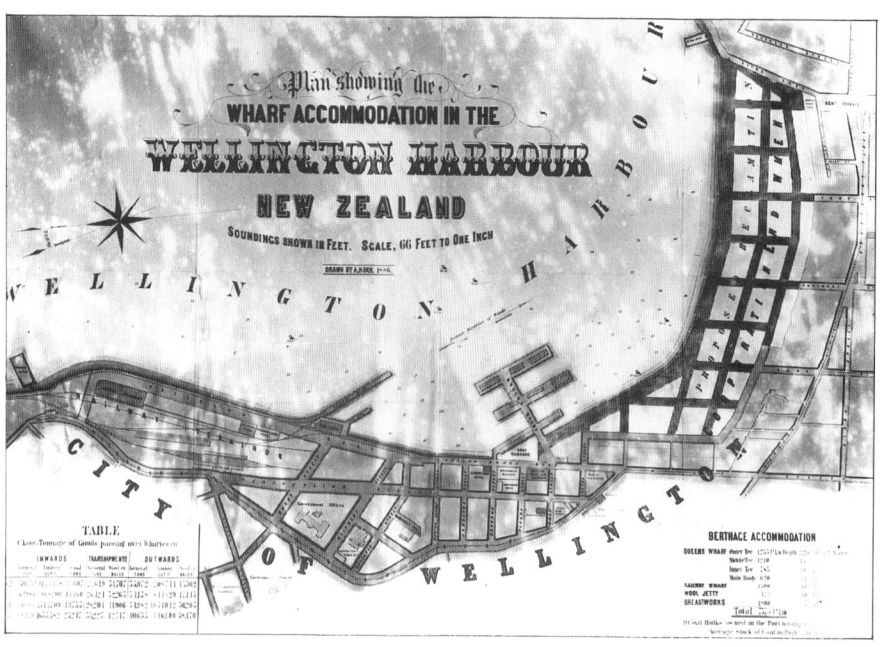

The Harbour Board's 1886 plan shows the reclamation of the railway yards complete but the Te Aro reclamation still proposed. That reclamation was a source of speech material for local politicians for years as the Harbour Board and City Council argued about control of the foreshore and who should have the profits from the sale of reclaimed land. The boat harbour between the inner tee of Queens Wharf and the seawall along Customhouse Quay gave shelter to the watermen's craft.
Wellington Maritime Museum

The view from Clifton Terrace, 1889. A wool ship loads at the Railway Wharf (left) while another is anchored nearby. Anchored in the harbour off Queens Wharf is a coal hulk, its high derricks allowing it to lift baskets of coal over the sides of steamers with much higher sides than the hulk. The post office's tower is still being rebuilt.
Alexander Turnbull Library

Just around the point from Te Aro, Oriental Bay was another world. While Te Aro was town, Oriental Bay was country. It was life at the seaside. The children on the left have paddled out to a piece of wreckage from the hulk *Eli Whitney*. The hulk was run down by the Union Company's steamer *Taupo* off Queens Wharf on a dark stormy night in 1877 with the loss of the hulk-keeper's wife and child. The remains of the ship were later blown up, but in 1887 there was still enough to interest the children of Oriental Bay.
Wellington Maritime Museum

Oriental Bay, 1889.
*Alexander Turnbull Library
(watercolour by Christopher Aubrey)*

2. Port and Capital City
Central Wellington, 1890-1939

Part of Chart BA 803 (first published 1906), showing port and foreshore development of inner Lambton Harbour.

It was the age of the steam engine, an age when coal was the universal fuel. In the background Wellington's commercial heart lies under a pall of smoke from factories, ships, and office and household fires. The two bowler-hatted gentlemen, perhaps taking their lunch break away from their desks, try their luck at fishing.
Alexander Turnbull Library (Christchurch Press collection)

![Queens Wharf photograph with sailing ships and steamers]

Queens Wharf, 3 pm on Tuesday 12 August 1890. Beyond shed D is the ornately decorated bow of Shaw Savill's steamship *Tainui*. With the *Arawa*, *Coptic*, *Doric* and *Ionic* she maintained Shaw Savill's half of the joint Shaw Savill-NZ Shipping Co main line mail service between New Zealand and the United Kingdom.

The *Tainui*'s design was a carryover from the days when steamers were sailing vessels with a little help from an engine. By the time she was built in 1884 most new steam vessels had straight stems. The *Tainui*, efficient as she was as a steamship, still carried sail. So did the coastal steamer *Kahu* in the foreground, where a sail can be seen neatly furled on the boom.

For 34 years from 1886 the *Kahu* carried cargo up and down the East Coast for Richardson & Co of Napier. Wellington had become a major transhipment port, and the *Kahu* was one of the many small vessels that fed it with wool and produce from the provinces, returning home with farm supplies and general merchandise from Wellington's importers and manufacturers.
Alexander Turnbull Library (Henry Wright)

Not far from Queens Wharf in Jervois Quay were the boating club sheds and skids. At the left is the Wellington Rowing Club, in the centre the Star Boating Club and at the right the headquarters of the Wellington Naval Volunteers. Activity is centred on the Star skids where officials in striped blazers are supervising the launching of the club's skiffs. Uniformed naval volunteers watch from their skids.
Wellington Maritime Museum

Queens Wharf 1892. In the foreground is Post Office Square. At the entrance to the wharf is the handsome new office of the Wellington Harbour Board, today occupied by the Wellington Maritime Museum. On the wharf are bales of wool awaiting shipment.
Wellington Maritime Museum

The view in the other direction, photographed on 26 March 1892. At the entrance to the wharf Harbour Board employees occupied small sentry boxes on each side of the gap, checking cargoes in and out.
Alexander Turnbull Library (Henry Wright)

Bales of wool and flax occupy much of the main section of Queens Wharf and extend onto at least one of the middle tees (right). The blackboard on the fence on the left lists vessels expected to arrive.

Queens Wharf was a place of continual bustle and congestion. There were insufficient berths and vessels often had to moor two abreast until a space could be found alongside. Dozens of small steamers shuttled back and forth between Wellington and ports north and south. In the centre of this photograph is a small steamer with a white-ringed black funnel, the colours of Levin & Co and of Eckford & Co of Blenheim, for whom they acted as agents. Levins were a major force in the flax trade, running a steamer from Foxton to Wellington and others from the Wairarapa coast and from Lyttelton via the Marlborough coast. *Wellington Maritime Museum*

Queens Wharf, the main entrance to the capital, was the scene of many state occasions as distinguished visitors came and went. This crowd turned out to greet Lord Ranfurly on his arrival in 1897 to take up his appointment as Governor of New Zealand. The leading horsemen of the Governor's procession have just passed the berthage board at the left of the flag-draped crane. To the right, the gap through the crowd is lined by a military guard of honour. *Wellington Maritime Museum*

Lord Ranfurly and the crowd have departed, and Queens Wharf gets on with its business on a wet windy day. The crane, devoid of its celebratory bunting, hoists cargo between wharf and hold. The berthage board in the foreground lists vessels berthed at Queens outer tee, Queens middle and inner tees, Railway Wharf and the Wool Jetty. The bookstall on the right is run by W.H. Smith. *Wellington Maritime Museum*

As members of the New Zealand First Contingent leave for South Africa on 21 October 1899 to fight the Boers they give a farewell salute to those they leave behind.
Wellington Maritime Museum

The little steamers serving the port were sometimes lucky enough to get a berth which provided a Harbour Board crane, but most of their cargo was loaded and unloaded with the ship's own gear powered by a steam donkey engine, with the assistance of crew members and wharfies. These men with their hand trolley pause for the photographer alongside the *Himitangi*, built in Scotland for Levin & Co in 1899. For years she ran in the trade between Wellington and Foxton, and Wellington and the Wairarapa coast.
Alexander Turnbull Library

When the Duke and Duchess of Cornwall and York, later to become King
George V and Queen Mary, visited Wellington in June 1901, Queens
Wharf was again dressed for the occasion. It was the second royal visit to
New Zealand. The first royal visitor, in 1869, was the Duke of Edinburgh,
then a captain in the Royal Navy and master of HMS *Galatea*.

The Duke and Duchess of Cornwall and York arrived from Auckland
on the *Ophir*, an Orient liner which had become a royal yacht for the tour.
While in Wellington they laid the foundation stones for the new town
hall and new NZ Railway offices, then sailed on to Lyttelton.
Wellington Maritime Museum (H. Bursewitz)

By 1904 the Victorian age was over. Women rode bicycles and Post Office
Square boasted a gaslight, with another at the wharf gate beyond. The
Harbour Board's new stores (left) separate Customhouse Quay from the
wharf. On the right are Queen's Chambers, which accommodated
Melbourne shipowners Huddart, Parker & Co; along with Henry Hughes,
patent attorney; and Munt, Cottrill & Co, who specialised in cartage to
and from the wharf. A sign on the new Harbour Board stores warns
Wellingtonians that if they are to be punctual they should carry a Stewart
Dawson watch.
Alexander Turnbull Library

Next to Queen's Chambers is the
imposing four-storeyed building of
W.M. Bannatyne & Co, shipping
agents and merchants (centre). On
the right, next to the Post Office, is
the Government Life Insurance
building. The trail of coal smoke is
probably from a steamship at
Queens Wharf.
Alexander Turnbull Library

Although Queen Victoria's reign was over, she was remembered by this
statue which replaced the gaslight. Huddart Parker's sign still adorns the
chimney on Queen's Chambers. Upstairs, above the office of the Westport
Coal Co, are rooms shared by J. Ilott's advertising agency and the Brett
Publishing Co, proprietors of a number of newspapers and magazines.
The sign on the Harbour Board's store no longer urges Wellingtonians to
carry a watch. It now recommends a game of billiards at the Federal Hall
in Manners Street.
Bowler hats were losing their place as the uniform of the man on the
move. The younger men about town, such as those in front of Queen's
Chambers, wore much lighter straw hats.
Alexander Turnbull Library

Before he completed his term as
Governor in 1904, Lord Ranfurly
took an active interest in a wide
variety of subjects from rugby to
the latest advances in technology.
Here the Wellington Harbour
Board's new steam fire engine is
demonstrated for his benefit.
Wellington Maritime Museum

Te Aro boasted a monument to industrial progress in the form of the City Council destructor with its towering chimneys. Reclamation continues, while the city lies beneath coal-age smog. The square building on the waterfront at Jervois Quay is the office and warehouse of the C & A Odlin Timber & Hardware Co. Ltd.
Alexander Turnbull Library

Handling coal was a back-breaking dirty business. In the hold of this collier men shovel loose coal into baskets which are then hoisted onto the coal hulk alongside and tipped into its hold. The canvas on the left collects coal spilled from the baskets. The process would be repeated later when the coal hulk was taken alongside a steamer and the baskets hoisted onto the steamer's deck to fill the stokehold.
Alexander Turnbull Library
(S.C. Smith)

In contrast to the garb of those who
shovelled coal are the starched
whites of the steward and
stewardess on this coastal steamer.
Although the small vessels trading
to the minor ports were essentially
cargo carriers they usually carried
up to a dozen passengers, and
sometimes the accommodation
was augmented by the squabs in
the saloon. But no matter how
small the vessel and how late the
hour of her sailing, food would be
served by smartly dressed crew
members. Meals were prepared on
a coal range in cramped quarters in
seas which were frequently
unfriendly, and many of the small
steamers were renowned for their
liquor cabinets rather than their
food.
Alexander Turnbull Library
(John Dickie)

A short stroll along the breastwork from Queens Wharf in the direction of
Railway Wharf was the jetty from which the harbour ferries set out for
Eastbourne, Days Bay and Miramar. The Wellington Steam Ferry Co Ltd
was formed in 1901 by J.H. Williams who had developed Days Bay as an
entertainment and picnic ground. In 1906 he sold out to the rival
Miramar Ferry Co, the combined fleets then running under the name of
Wellington Harbour Ferries with E.G.F. Zohrab as manager. At the wharf
is the ferry company's *Countess*, and behind her the company's tug *Pilot*.
Alexander Turnbull Library

The arrival of the mail steamer from the United Kingdom was sure to attract a crowd to the wharf. This ship's eye view taken in 1908 shows rather more official crowd control than normal. The ship carried a particularly important passenger: Sir William Hall-Jones, former Prime Minister, returning after a period as New Zealand High Commissioner in London.
Alexander Turnbull Library

Men at work, pick-and-shovel style. This plate-laying gang is maintaining the lines on the Railway Wharf.
Alexander Turnbull Library

In 1913 the Eastbourne Borough Council took over the ferry service, proudly proclaiming the first "municipalisation" of a ferry service in the Southern Hemisphere. On the left is the ferry service office, which was also the borough office for some years. Borough councillors held their meetings in the upstairs rooms, continuing with unofficial business as they crossed the harbour. The borough bought Wellington Harbour Ferries' steamers *Duchess* and *Cobar* while the company's manager bought the tugs and small harbour craft.

At right, with the tall funnel painted with two white rings, is E.G.F. Zohrab's tug *Karaka*. Behind her, at the Lyttelton steamer express berth, is the Union Company's *Mararoa*. In the centre, the funnel with the dark spot is that of a Blackball Coal Co collier. Her mast, with the distinctive high derricks, can be seen above the lifeboat in front of the *Mararoa*'s funnel. In the foreground is the *Janie Seddon*, usually described as the Defence Department steamer. For half a century she chugged about Wellington Harbour on errands which included taking soldiers to and from Fort Dorset.
Alexander Turnbull Library (S.C.Smith)

When one of the Harbour Board's new petrol-engine tractors was demonstrated in 1919, flax was still a major export. Despite the introduction of tractors, horses and drays were to be a common sight on the wharves for a long time.
Wellington Maritime Museum (Palmer & Mahood)

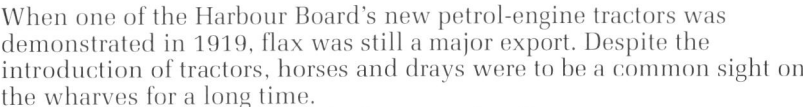

After the Great War of 1914-18 there was a new wave of migration to New Zealand, encouraged by a 1920 decision to accept 10,000 people a year from the United Kingdom, the cost of passage being shared between the New Zealand and United Kingdom governments. Here, immigrants disembark from Shaw Savill's *Waimana* in April 1921. The subsidised migration scheme continued until 1927.
Wellington Maritime Museum

Gradually motor transport drove horses from the wharves, although it took nearly three decades to do so. C. Webster, general carrier, was one of many who earned his living from the waterfront. He must have done better than many — this truck is labelled "No. 93".
Alexander Turnbull Library

Wellington's wharves in the thirties, when sea transport was at its peak and the aeroplane still a novelty.

At the Eastbourne ferry wharf are the *Cobar* (left) and the *Muritai*. At the Inter-Island Wharf (the sign on the shed says Lyttelton Wharf) are the Lyttelton express steamers *Maori* and *Wahine*. Beyond are the funnels of the Home ships. For half a century the Conference Lines — a cartel of half a dozen shipping companies — controlled the route to Europe. Not until the advent of containers did their monopoly crumble. In the twenties and thirties they were masters of the seas, providing a liner service in return for the ability to set rates.

In the foreground on the right is the Union Company's harbour tug *Natone*. On the left, tucked into the corner in front of the *Cobar* is the Defence Department's *Janie Seddon*.
Alexander Turnbull Library

Liner day. The Harbour Board's pilot launch *Uta* hovering beneath the bows of one of the New Zealand Line's famous "Rangis" — the *Rangitane*, *Rangitiki* or *Rangitata*.
Alexander Turnbull Library

Customhouse Quay. The Post Office is on the left, the Government Life Insurance building in the next block, and the Union Steam Ship Co's head office beyond. The newsagent's shop which has replaced the statue of Queen Victoria in the middle of Post Office Square is roped off, perhaps to protect newly planted grass. In the foreground, taxi cabs await custom.
Alexander Turnbull Library

The nearest thing to an aerial view in 1924: a panoramic photograph taken from the wireless station. On the left the Pipitea reclamation is covered with wool stores and warehouses. The foreshore has essentially taken the shape it will retain until the advent of the container age.
Wellington Maritime Museum (S.C. Smith)

In August 1925 a United States fleet visited Wellington, crowding the harbour with majestic men-of-war and the streets with sailors. On the left are the early stages of the Thorndon reclamation, with coal hulks moored off it, out of the way of harbour traffic.
Alexander Turnbull Library (Crown Studio)

While the fleet was in port there was an endless round of dinners, dances, parties and receptions. Entertaining the Americans became the city's major occupation. The Harbour Board's shed 17 was converted to a giant dormitory so that sailors who had shore leave did not have to shuttle back and forth to their ships. To show their appreciation for Wellington's hospitality the visiting fleet staged a searchlight display.
Alexander Turnbull Library (Leslie Hinge)

▷ In 1929 Richard E. Byrd called at Wellington on his way back from to Antarctica where he had made the first flight to the South Pole. Here his Curtis Wright Condor aircraft is on show at Pipitea Wharf. Then, as now, sponsorship was necessary. Shell Oil, providers of Byrd's fuel, lined up their transport fleet to show their support.
Alexander Turnbull Library

Thorndon reclamation, November 1925. Before the pumping of mud and shifting of spoil began the outer line was delineated by the building of the breastwork seen here. In the background on the left, between the hills and the sea, are the warehouses of the petroleum companies, with signs proclaiming some of the brands of the day: Shell, Plume, Laurel and Big Tree. In 1925 Wellington's petroleum needs arrived in cases, not in tankers. Although oil storage tanks were built at Miramar in 1921, the first bulk oil shipment did not arrive until January 1926. In the foreground is the Railways' coal stockpile.
Wellington Maritime Museum (Palmer & Mahood)

In March 1930 Thorndon was still being reclaimed. Nearly five years of pumping mud have made their mark, but there's a long way to go. There are still petroleum warehouses, and above them are the wool stores of the major stock and station agents. The large store with the ridged roof in the right foreground belongs to Dalgety & Co.
Wellington Maritime Museum (Robson & Boyer)

Downtown Wellington from the air, January 1930. Lambton Quay is on the far right, Customhouse Quay in the centre. The new Huddart Parker Building is prominent in Post Office Square, occupying the site of the old Queen's Chambers. On Lambton Quay is the imposing department store of Kirkcaldie & Stains. Near the bottom right is the Dominion Farmers' Institute.

At the Inter-Island Ferry Wharf at bottom left is the Union Company's *Maori*. At the Eastbourne ferry jetty are the *Muritai* (outer berth) and the *Duchess*. At Queens Wharf inner, alongside the Harbour Board office, is the Anchor Shipping Company's cargo steamer *Kaitoa*. Astern of her is their *Arahura* which ran in the nightly Wellington–Nelson passenger service from 1925 until 1949.
Wellington Maritime Museum (Evening Post)

Interest in aviation was intense as pioneer aviators notched up one endurance feat after another. In February 1930, not long after Byrd's visit, Francis Chichester came to town. On 11 February he and his aircraft — minus wings — were paraded through the streets, and here in Post Office Square Wellingtonians have turned out in force. Chichester rides on the truck, a Scammell provided by Shell whose claim to fame, "Chichester Chose Shell", is prominently displayed. Senior staff of the Harbour Board are out on the balcony to watch and a photographer is perched precariously on the roof.
Wellington Maritime Museum (S.C. Smith)

When word was received at the Harbour Board office on 28 December 1931 that the Jubilee Floating Dock in tow of the Dutch tugs *Witte Zee* (left) and *Zwarte Zee* was approaching Port Nicholson, members of the Board and their friends set out in the tug *Natone* to welcome their new acquisition. The tow created a new record: 14,109 nautical miles from Newcastle-on-Tyne in 167 days. The dock was put through its paces in April 1932 when the New Zealand Shipping Company's liner *Ruahine* was borrowed for a lifting trial.
Alexander Turnbull Library

Well into the thirties horses and carts were still hard at work on the wharves, holding their own against the Harbour Board tractors with their long lines of low-slung trailers, and the lorries of the carrying companies. These draught horses await instructions alongside a Munt Cottrill lorry.
Alexander Turnbull Library

Wellington continued to thrive as an export port, shipping produce from its own freezing works and transhipping wool, dairy produce and other primary produce. Here the New Zealand Shipping Company's *Rangitane* loads barrels of tallow for the United Kingdom. In 1937 wool was the biggest export — 48,820 tons worth 5.65 million pounds. Butter and cheese were next, worth 4.8 million pounds. A third of the wool and nearly half the butter and cheese were transhipped after arriving from other ports in coastal vessels. The rest arrived by rail or road.
Alexander Turnbull Library

Customhouse Quay, April 1939.
The bicycle, and the Baby Austin
and trailer are parked outside the
Government Life building. The
Huddart Parker building is in the
centre.
Alexander Turnbull Library

Bright lights shine on the wharves
as cargo is loaded onto Huddart
Parker's *Wanganella*, which ran in
the Sydney–Wellington/Auckland
service. In 1947, on her first
post-war civilian voyage, she ran
onto Barretts Reef and remained
there for 18 days before being
hauled off.
Alexander Turnbull Library

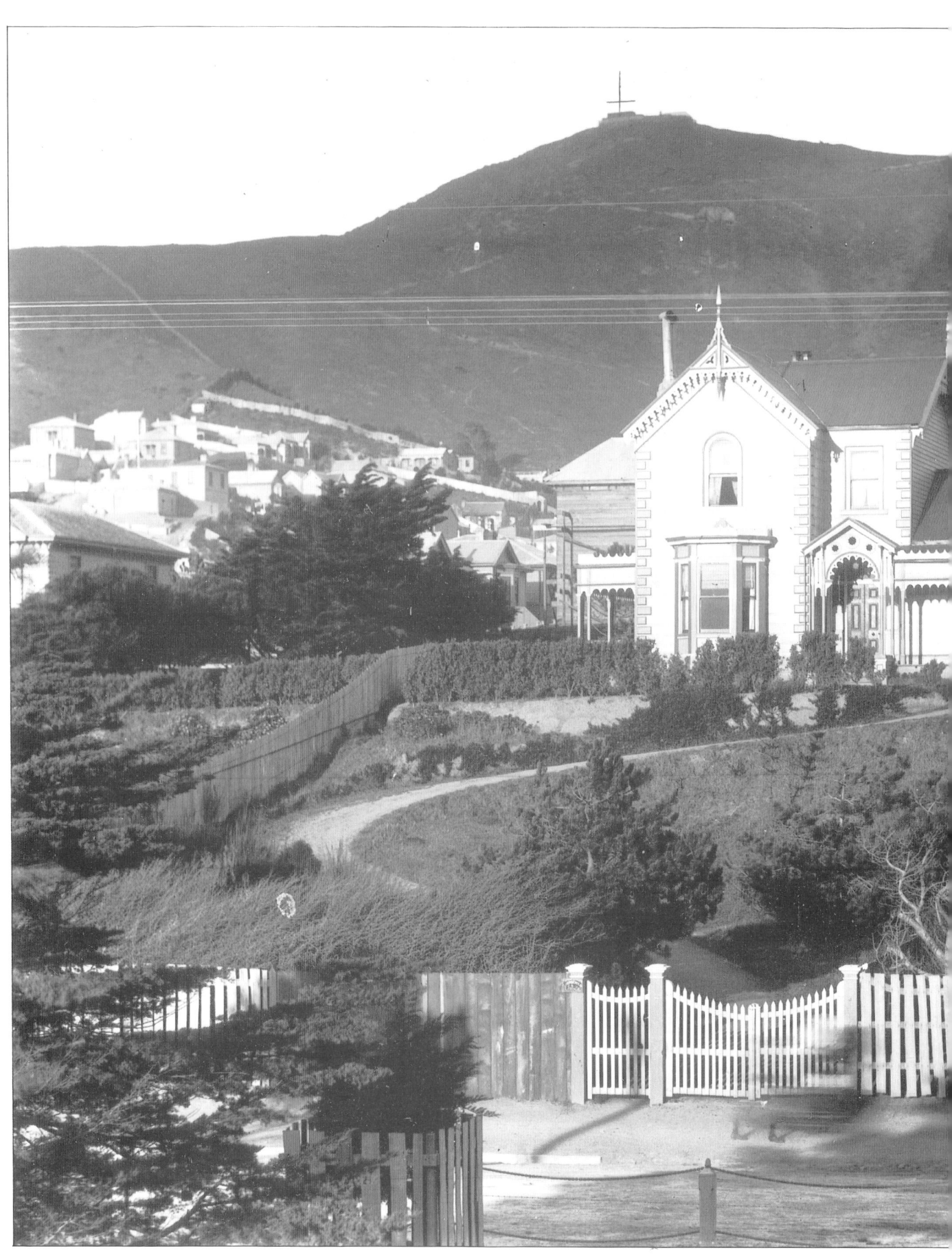

While the city centre was being developed, reclaimed, built and re-built, and while houses gradually crept up the slopes towards Kelburn and Wadestown and spread out of the valleys onto the spurs, the coast and the hills at the far end of Te Aro were gaining in popularity. Mount Victoria, with its unsurpassed views, attracted those who could run a horse and cart or afford a hansom cab, or who just enjoyed a walk. Here, in the 1890s, 18 Edge Hill on Mount Victoria overlooks the magnificent waters of Port Nicholson.
Alexander Turnbull Library

At sea level, at the far end of Oriental Bay from the city, was the Oriental Bay Kiosk. Although not always used as a tea kiosk and hall, it was a landmark for more than half a century.
Alexander Turnbull Library

The Kiosk offered meals in elegant surroundings resplendent with pillars, pot plants, high ceilings, and a bevy of starched waitresses.
Alexander Turnbull Library

The city side of Mount Victoria, with Oriental Bay around the point to the left. By 1910 the lower slopes had become crowded. Houses in Roxburgh Street at the top of the cliff extended their land area by propping their verandahs and front yards on posts. On the upper left McFarlane Street can be seen running along the cliff top. The houses to the right of centre at the back are in Kennedy Street.
Alexander Turnbull Library (S.C. Smith)

Roxburgh Street runs behind the houses on the clifftop in the foreground. Parallel with it, further back, is Hawker Street. Towards the left the short tongue of Duke Street protrudes downhill from Hawker Street.
Alexander Turnbull Library (S.C. Smith)

The slopes of Mount Victoria were still virtually treeless and uninhabited near the top, but down towards Kent and Cambridge Terraces large houses lined the streets. These had a view, and were owned by clerks and small businessmen. They were much larger homes than the workmen's cottages that were jammed into the Te Aro flats until more and bigger factories and warehouses squeezed them out.
Majoribanks Street runs from Kent Terrace across the centre of the picture. Off it, beyond the school, Lipman Street runs through to Levy Street. The tarsealed school playground at the beginning of Oriental Parade is today occupied by the fire station.
Alexander Turnbull Library (S.C. Smith)

The first seaplane to visit Wellington, in 1921, was moored in the Clyde Quay boat harbour, where local residents came to gaze at the frail machine. It was flown by George Bolt, who pioneered airmail in New Zealand in his Boeing seaplane, from the New Zealand Flying School based at Mission Bay in Auckland. The Union Company steamer is berthed at Clyde Quay wharf, constructed for the coal and timber trades.
Alexander Turnbull Library (S.C. Smith)

In the late 1880s and into the 1890s the Port Nicholson Yacht Club's keeler fleet grew, and there was a clear need for shelter for small craft. The Harbour Board decided to build a boat harbour alongside Clyde Quay where the road began to round the first point on its way to Oriental Bay. In 1904 Young & Sellar were awarded a contract to build shed foundations and skids. One of the conditions of the permit was that the roof level of the sheds would not protrude above the low wall running along the seaward side of Clyde Quay. This would preserve the view from the waterfront. By 1907 the Harbour Board had built 24 sheds but was having difficulty finding tenants. The rentals, ranging from seven pounds ten shillings to 23 pounds a year, were considered by boat owners to be far too high.

Here the sheds crouch beneath the wall as a city-bound tram passes by. The houses at Oriental Parade level (from the centre to the right) were built by Wakelin in 1900.
Alexander Turnbull Library (S.C. Smith)

Eventually the Harbour Board convinced boatowners that its sheds were good value, but it took a long time. The original 24 sheds sat for 20 years before any more were built. The Port Nicholson Yacht Club moved its headquarters from Thorndon to Clyde Quay and the boat harbour there became the base for Wellington's serious yachting.
Alexander Turnbull Library (S.C. Smith)

The Clyde Quay boat harbour in January 1939 as the fleet prepares for a day's racing. It was still the coal age; two hulks are berthed at Clyde Quay Wharf. At Queens Wharf (top right) can be seen the stern of the Union Company's trans-Tasman liner *Awatea*.
Alexander Turnbull Library (Free Lance collection)

Beyond the boat harbour — and in existence well before the boat harbour — were the Te Aro baths. At this session at the baths in 1908 officials sit on a small table on planks between beams. Hats are in fashion: cloth caps and straw hats for the men, flower-bedecked creations for the women.
Alexander Turnbull Library
(S.C. Smith)

A little further along the coast even signs on the wooden drainpipes showed evidence that this was the commercial age. The woman seated on the "You can depend on Rudge-Whitworths" drain is dressed to the nines, Edwardian style, with a flyaway hat and a fur stole, complete with dangling tail. On the left a path zig-zags down a retaining wall of ferro-cement, a commodity which had just gained universal acceptance and was being mixed by the hundreds of tons for bridges and wharves.
Alexander Turnbull Library
(Price collection)

At the far end of the bay Carlton Gore Road sweeps majestically up to the heights of Mount Victoria. In 1926 it was a broad and newly-sealed accessway for the wave of new homes built on the slopes.
Alexander Turnbull Library

Oriental Bay, 1932. This was Wellington's city beach, a place close to the centre where Wellingtonians could go for a swim and sit in the sun. Days Bay was still popular, but involved a ferry trip. Titahi Bay and Plimmerton were a long way to drive on roads that were inclined to clothe the traveller in dust.
Alexander Turnbull Library
(S.C. Smith)

For all the sunshine and sparkling waters, Port Nicholson can cut up rough. When it does, owners of small craft are thankful for the concrete walls that keep their vessels safe in the Clyde Quay boat harbour. Here the concrete viewing area by Clyde Quay Wharf gets a white one over the top.
Alexander Turnbull Library (Evening Post *collection*)

Wellington had had a number of visits by enterprising airmen from overseas and scheduled air travel within New Zealand had been a fact since 1930. Cook Strait Airways ran services from Wellington to Blenheim and Nelson from 1935 and Union Airways began in 1936. When Imperial Airways' *Centaurus* arrived in 1937 it seemed that the trans-Tasman liners might soon have competition. It was not until after the Second World War, however, that commercial services linked Australia and New Zealand.
Alexander Turnbull Library (Evening Post *collection*)

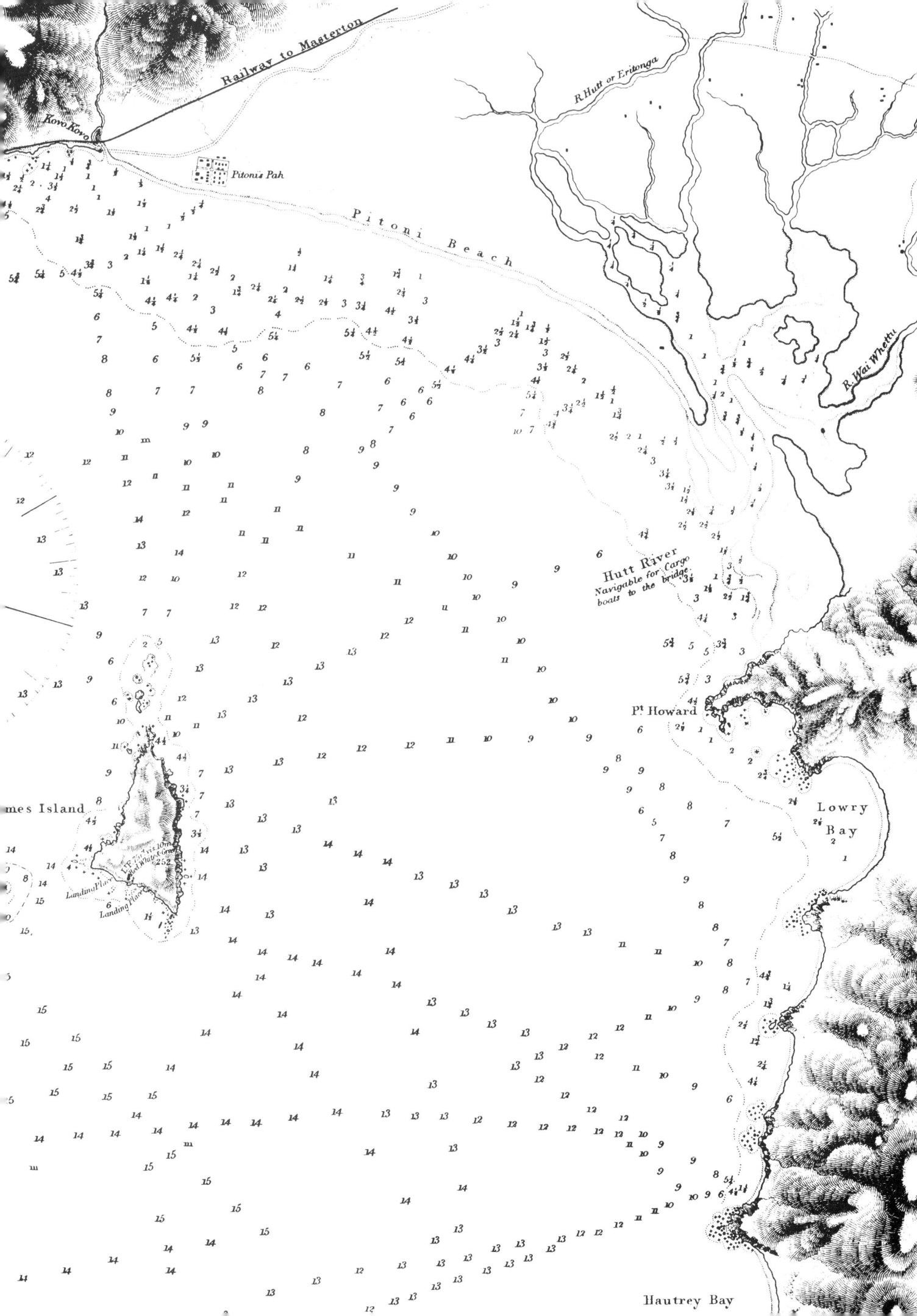

Railway to Masterton

R. Hutt or Eritonga

Koro Koro

Pitoni's Pah

Pitoni Beach

R. Wai Whetta

Hutt River
Navigable for Cargo
boats to the bridge

Pt Howard

Lowry
Bay

...mes Island

Landing Place
Landing Place

Hautrey Bay

3. The Shores of Port Nicholson
Pencarrow Head to Eastbourne, Petone, and Kaiwharawhara

Part of Chart BA 1423 (1856), showing northern and eastern shores of Port Nicholson.

Pencarrow lighthouse, sentinel of the harbour entrance. The first Pencarrow lighthouse was built only after a decade of agitation by the merchants of the town, who were increasingly concerned about the dangers to their ships and cargoes as they made their way through the entrance in dead of night. The lighthouse was a small wooden affair, more of a house with a light than a lighthouse.

The second Pencarrow lighthouse, shown here, is cast iron. It arrived from England in kitset form, and was boated ashore and landed on the beach just outside the Heads where it began shining its light on 1 January 1859. Now a historic place, it ceased functioning as a lighthouse when Baring Head lighthouse was commissioned in 1935. Pencarrow is now marked by a low-level light which was built in 1906.

In this photograph, taken about 1913, a group of Harbour Board employees pose on the balcony. The Harbour Board took over management from the Government in 1912.
Wellington Maritime Museum (A.P. Godber)

Outside the Heads, to the east, is Fitzroy Bay, a gravel-faced sweep of beach inhabited by birdlife and the small creatures of the seashore. In the days of sailing ships, getting into Port Nicholson was often a difficult business. Until the 1890s there was no steam tug at the port, but ships were sometimes taken under tow by passing steamers if they happened to be in the right place at the right time and the steamer's masters were interested in earning extra revenue.

Frequently vessels beat about Cook Strait waiting for a wind that allowed them to enter the Heads. Sometimes they were blown far out to sea or up the coast, to return another day. Sometimes they kept too close, and were wrecked. Schooners and ketches could be off and away with a change in the wind, but Fitzroy Bay caused many an anxious moment for masters of some of the bigger square-rigged vessels. Barques and larger ships took time to go about and some became embayed, trapped in the confines of the bay and unable to work their way out no matter how much they tacked. And some of the ships that became embayed went ashore in Fitzroy Bay.

Here a trans-Tasman liner passes Fitzroy Bay, making for Pencarrow Head and the harbour entrance.
Alexander Turnbull Library (Robinson & Boyer)

Despite the light, and despite steam propulsion, ships still came ashore. In a howling gale and driving rain the master of the Federal-Houlder-Shire steamer *Devon* got his lights confused. His ship ran hard ashore on the night of 25 August 1913 and was soon battered to pieces, her wreckage spread along the beach near the Pencarrow low light. With a great deal of difficulty a line was run ashore and the *Devon*'s crew members taken off safely.
Wellington Maritime Museum (A.P. Godber)

Eastbourne has always been a world of its own, a harbour's width apart from Wellington and its city ways. Italian fishermen settled in Rona Bay in the early 1890s. By 1903 they had been joined by a small number of families as limited development spread around the bluff from Days Bay, which had become Wellington's playground as the landowner J.H. Williams poured time, imagination and money into it. The Rona Bay Sanitorium and Steam Ferry Co Ltd was formed in 1903 but gained neither a sanitorium nor a steam ferry. One of its promoters, Bartolo Russo, did open an accommodation house. When Williams eventually sold out and the subdivision of Days Bay began, it was only a matter of time before Rona Bay had its own wharf and became a ferry stop.

Here the ferry *Cobar* glides into her berth as morning commuters crowd the end of the wharf. On the left is the shop of C. Russell, general storekeeper and provision merchant. In front on the left is the home of S. Jackson, plumber and drainlayer.
Alexander Turnbull Library (S.C. Smith)

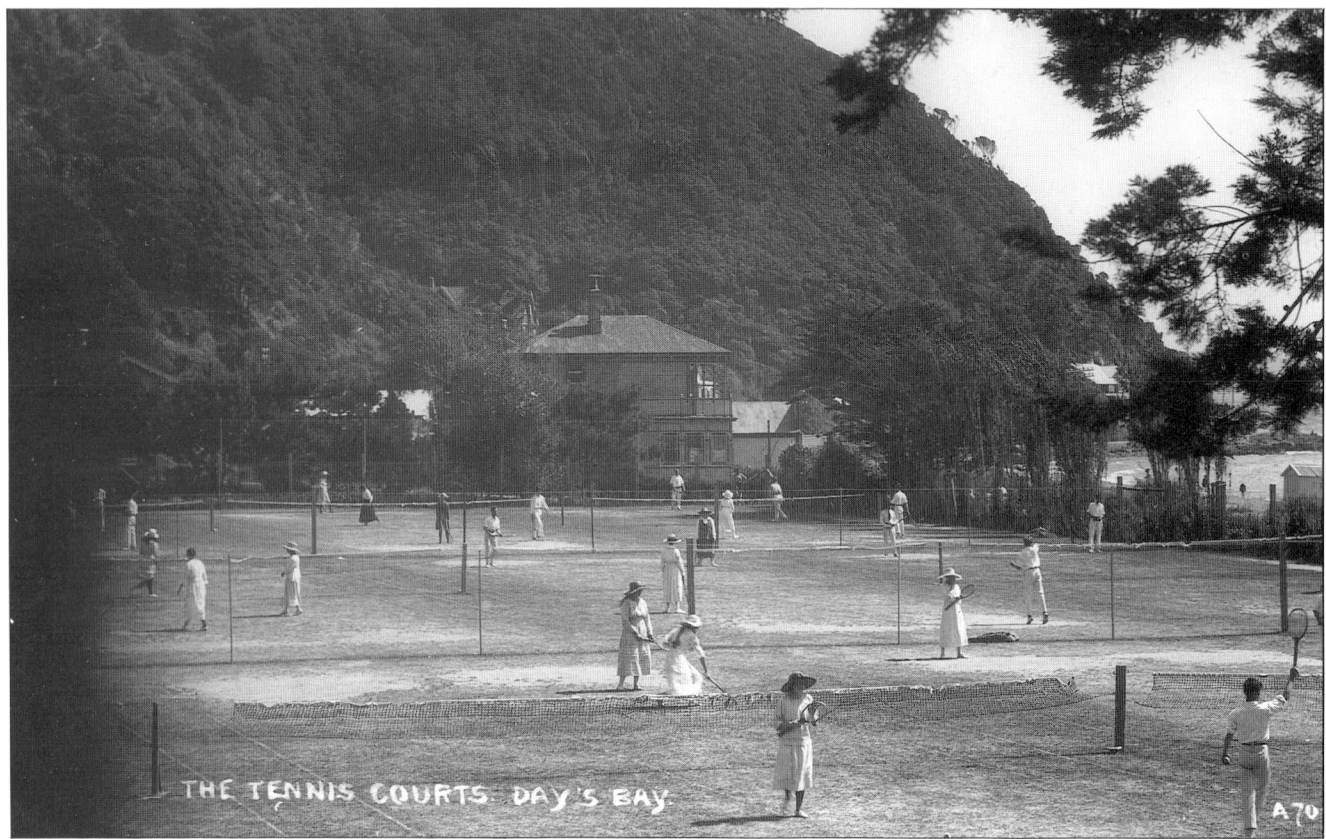

THE TENNIS COURTS DAY'S BAY.   A70

Tennis time. Days Bay accommodation house is in the background.

Days Bay was bought by J.H. Williams in November 1894 for 1000 pounds. Williams was the son of Captain W.R. Williams, a sailing ship man who had come ashore to found a successful coal dealing business. Captain Williams became a mine owner and the proprietor of the Black Diamond Line of steamships. When he sold out to the Union Steam Ship Company J.H. Williams put his efforts into the development of a harbour towage business and also ran excursions to Lowry Bay. When Days Bay became available he bought it, spent another 1100 pounds on a wharf, and ran the first excursion there on Labour Day 1895. He never looked back.

During the next five years Williams poured money into the project, then sold it and his ferries *Duco* and *Duchess* to a new public company, the Wellington Steam Ferry Co. He became its managing director. More ferries were built or bought, an accommodation house was built, tennis courts were laid and there were picnic grounds, sports grounds, and walking tracks through the bush.
Auckland Public Library

Williams' first major construction at Days Bay was the pavilion, which became the centrepoint of all social occasions in the Bay. The pavilion was for a time the scene of mid-week concerts, and the ticket included ferry travel from Wellington, the concert, supper, and the ride home.

Here the chute behind the pavilion is in full swing. Crinoline skirts and large hats were no handicap to a determined young lady of the Edwardian era when she wanted to ride the chute. The queue stretches down the ramp while the brakeman (bottom left) controls the speed. The tennis courts are at top left.
Alexander Turnbull Library (S.C. Smith)

Days Bay was the scene of great feats of showmanship. Here Captain Noah Jonassen, "the Ariel King", prepares to ascend in his hot air balloon. Anyone in command of a craft seemed to be a captain, just as anyone who appeared on stage and said witty things was referred to as a professor.
Auckland Public Library

The Pavilion. Nobody in Wellington asked "Which pavilion?". There was only one. Here visitors promenade or enjoy cups of tea. Those looking for something more exciting visit the castle and sideshows, off to the left. The game of cricket being conducted on the right is a gentlemanly affair, probably with son bowling to dad and vice versa. There wasn't sufficient room for batsmen to show off. To do that they moved to the cricket ground next door.
Auckland Public Library

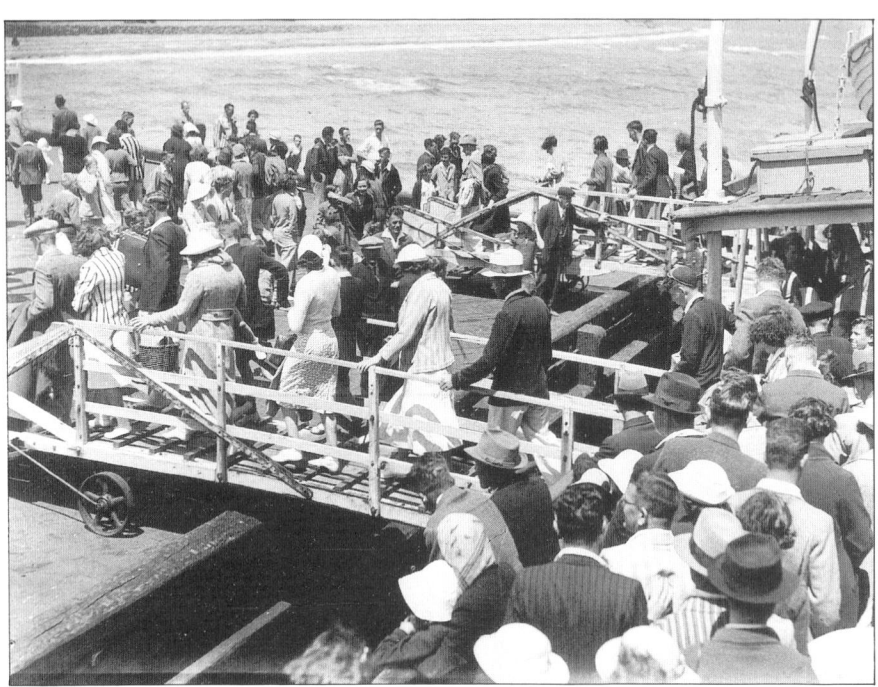

A day at the beach, 1930s style. Striped blazers are very much in evidence, on both men and women. In the middle, wearing a white hat, is Charles Bishop, for many years town clerk, manager of the ferries, and later mayor of Eastbourne. Captain W. Reid, once a master in the Eastbourne fleet and now a wharfinger in his semi-retirement, is beyond Bishop, tending the far gangway.

Days Bay was the one Wellington resort that lasted the distance. With the advent of the motor car, and the building of roads and tramlines, more beaches became accessible, more picnic spots were developed. Days Bay in the thirties had become a beach in front of Williams Park and the park had begun to be encompassed by houses, but it was still "The Bay".
J. Gibb (photograph by Charles P.S. Boyer)

When they got to the beach they lay in the sun, promenaded, chatted, flirted, went walking, had cups of tea, or in the best tradition of the thirties surreptitiously pulled something stronger — and socially more daring — from their beach bags. A few swam, but most kept their clothes and their hats on. Not a lot of notice was taken of the warning sign beside the stream that sometimes became a drain.

At the wharf are the *Cobar* and *Muritai*. The *Muritai* provided Eastbourne's commuters with far better facilities than they'd ever had before, but cost so much to run in her early days that she was laid up most of the time and only put on the service for special occasions.
Alexander Turnbull Library (S.C. Smith)

Before Days Bay took over, Lowry Bay was Wellington's picnic spot. From the late 1850s, initially a couple of times a year, small coastal steamers would be chartered by a body such as the Oddfellows for a public picnic at some point around the harbour. Small craft such as this one ferried visitors to shore. Sometimes a punt was towed across and became a temporary landing stage. This seems to be a gentlemen only occasion — or perhaps the women have already been carried well above the high tide mark.

Lowry Bay was owned by the Bell family who readily made their grounds available. Williams built a wharf there and his ships carried thousands of passengers on excursions until he bought Days Bay and shifted his attention there.
Alexander Turnbull Library (Bell collection)

Lowry Bay, 12 February 1888. The summer holidays have ended. School is back, the excursion season is over, except for a brief flurry at Easter. At left is The Lodge, at right The Ngaio.
Alexander Turnbull Library (Halse collection)

With Williams and his thousands
of day trippers now around the
corner at Days Bay, Lowry Bay was
once more a place where a family
could pitch tents and be away from
it all. These campers at Lowry Bay
in 1896 must have edged their
horses and conveyances around
the rough track from the Hutt
Valley.
*Alexander Turnbull Library
(Peterson collection)*

In 1906 Lowry Bay was chopped
up into house-sized sections and
auctioned. It was the age of
"development". With Williams no
longer at the helm of the
Wellington Steam Ferry Co, Days
Bay was being subdivided. Rona
Bay was too. On the Miramar
Peninsula on the far side of the
harbour it was a race between
competing landowners to carve up
and sell, sell, sell.
    Although the map shows the
location of Lowry Bay in relation
to the booming industrial area of
Petone, access was not by road
from the Hutt Valley, but by bus to
the Days Bay wharf.
Alexander Turnbull Library

PLAN OF
Lowry Bay
ESTATE

103 Ideal Seaside Sections. 103
To be sold by PUBLIC AUCTION on
Wednesday, Dec. 5th, 1906,
At 2.30 p.m., by
William H. Turnbull and Co,
At their Auction Rooms,
3, PANAMA STREET, WELLINGTON.

LOCALITY PLAN

THIS Magnificent Seaside Estate has for many
years been justly recognised as absolutely
the best residential property within the limits of
the Wellington Harbour.   For many years the
people of Wellington have longed for the oppor-
tunity now presented to them to acquire building
sites in this delightful marine retreat, which com-
bines forest clad hills and valleys with one of the
finest stretches of sandy beach to be found in New
Zealand.   More than half of the sections to be
offered have direct access to the sea, and the
most artistic imagination could not depict more
beautiful scenery than that presented by some of
these most charming and picturesque bush gullies
with their rippling water frontages and sandy
beaches.

LOWRY BAY
Is the Safest and Best Sheltered in the Harbour
for
BOATING,
        BATHING,
                FISHING,
                        and YACHTING.

Picnic, Boating, Yachting and Camping parties
have long used this Ideal seaside pleasure ground
in preference to any of the other beauty spots
around Wellington.

SPECIALLY EASY TERMS.
        10 per cent. cash,
        5 per cent. in six months,
        5 per cent. in twelve months.
The balance may remain for TEN YEARS.
    Interest on unpaid purchase money, 5 per cent.
per annum.

Daily 'Bus Service.
Arrangements have been made for a morning and evening
Bus Service to be run between the Day's Bay Wharf and the
Lowry Bay Estate, thus placing this superb seaside resort upon
equal terms with the other suburbs on this side of the harbour.

Free 'Bus Trips from Day's Bay
for intending purchasers to view the sections will be made
Every Wednesday and Saturday
to date of sale.
Every section is pegged, flagged and numbered.
Our representatives will be on the ground each day to assist
prospective buyers to inspect the property.

Wm. H. Turnbull & Co.,
    Auctioneers,
        3, Panama Street.

H. P. HANIFY,
Licensed Surveyor
WELLINGTON

Scale 132 feet to 1 inch

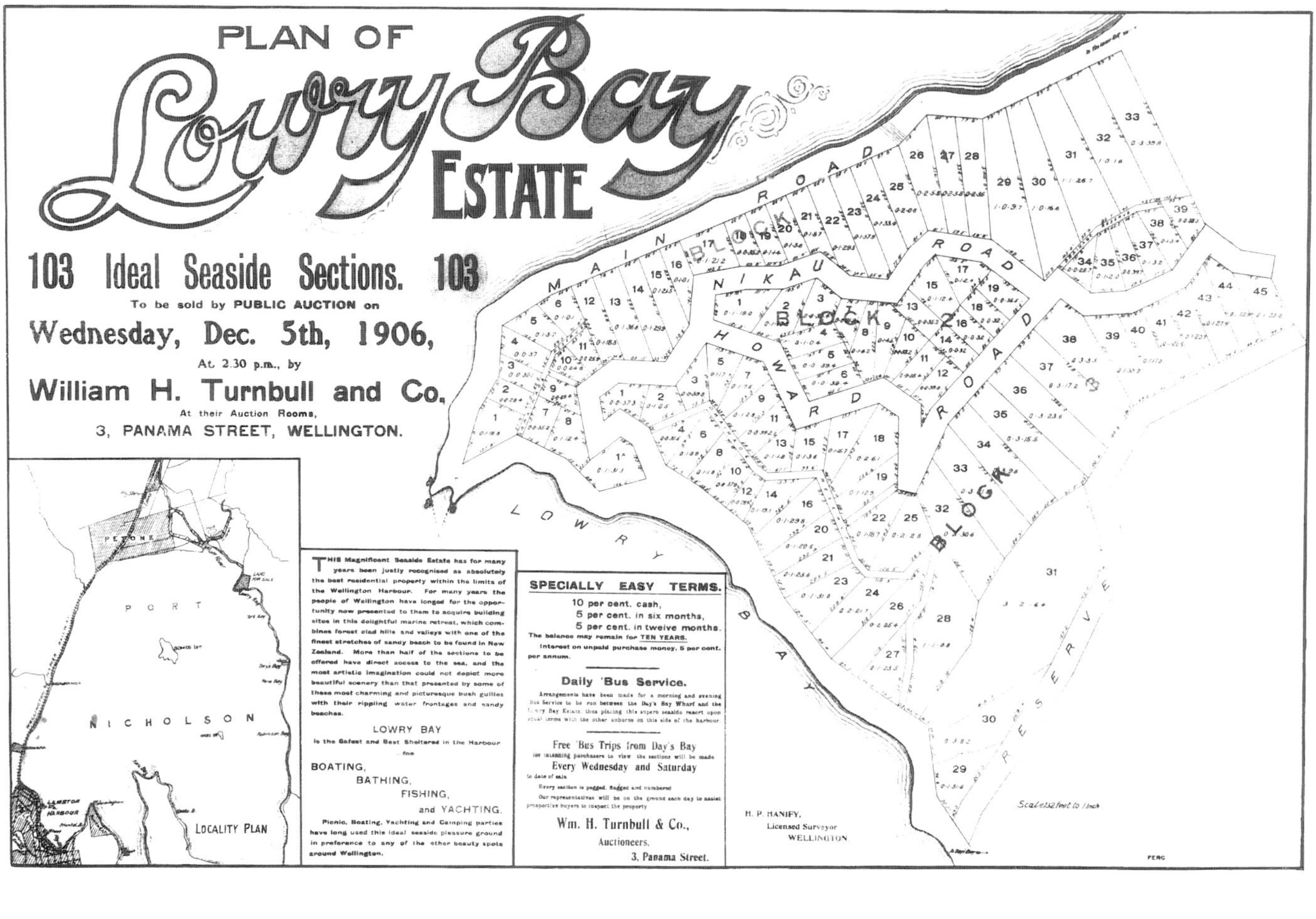

Between the bays and the rapidly industrialising Petone area was Point Howard. It wasn't particularly notable; just a lump of land that got in the way of the road. In the 1920s oil fuel was taking over, just as steam had revolutionised manufacturing and commerce in its heyday.

As the car population grew, as the diesel engine's influence spread, and as industrial concerns switched from steam to oil, the oil business boomed. A new home for it had to be found, and this was at Point Howard.

In this March 1929 photograph Point Howard shows only one sign of progress: the cut through the hill for the road to the bays. The old road goes through a small cut, and the cartroad goes around the edge. *Wellington Maritime Museum (Leslie Hinge)*

On the Petone side of Point Howard work had already begun on site preparation for the Texas Company's oil installation. The Texas Company occupied five and a half acres (2.25 hectares). More of the hill was carved away and a long jetty was built, reaching out to deep water. The first tanker to use the new wharf was the Texas Company's *Australia* on 20 January 1930. *Wellington Maritime Museum (Leslie Hinge)*

Petone beach in the early 1880s. At the left is the road to Wellington. At the end of the long jetty extending from the Gear Meat Company's works is their freezing hulk *Jubilee.* Behind the beach are the houses of the workers at the meat works and the other industrial undertakings being established in the area. The Hutt Valley was still largely farmland. *Alexander Turnbull Library*

Petone wharf about 1914, drays awaiting their turn to be filled with coal from the wicker baskets swung by the ship's derricks. The amount of coal unloaded at suburban wharves in 1913 and 1914 increased to more than 20,000 tonnes a year, compared with less than 400 tonnes in 1911. *Wellington Maritime Museum (A.P. Godber)*

Petone beach is hardly the sort of beach to feature on postcards, but a beach is still a beach, especially when summer comes and it's just down the road. In 1924, these swimmers, mostly children, enjoy the water. To the right of centre is a raft used as a swimmers' rendezvous. In the background is Somes Island. *Alexander Turnbull Library*

Hutt Valley in 1934, a booming dormitory town soon to be a city in its own right.
Alexander Turnbull Library
(Evening Post)

These small boats were typical of the pleasure craft on Wellington Harbour from the earliest days of pakeha settlement. The clinker-built sailing dinghy on the left was similar to those used to link Petone and Lambton Harbour in the 1840s, and was a design much favoured by watermen for at least 60 years after that. This yachting party paused for a swim in May 1888. It must have been a long summer! Somes Island is in the background.
Alexander Turnbull Library
(Halse collection)

Where Ngauranga gorge met the coast a stream trickled down to the sea. It was a scene of rural tranquillity when S.C. Brees passed by with his sketchbook about 1843.
Alexander Turnbull Library

The Ngauranga gorge, roughly half way between Wellington and the Hutt Valley, was a convenient stopping point for travellers on foot, a resting place for horses. Horses and carts, and behind them a stagecoach, wait outside Clapham's Inn in 1875. The railway line at left was constructed in the previous year.
Alexander Turnbull Library

When these stage coaches paused at Ngauranga in the 1890s they were well away from home. Normally they were engaged on Cobb & Co's run to Newtown (fare threepence). Cobb & Co's name appeared on hundreds of coaches in all parts of the country, but the company was not as all-pervading as it seemed. Its name was held in such high regard that it was borrowed by coach owners everywhere. With this number of people on board there was little room for luggage, so the event was probably a day trip. The group is segregated: men on the front coaches, a few women towards the rear.
Alexander Turnbull Library

The train stands still, in line with the Ngauranga station staff, all holding their positions for the photographer.
Alexander Turnbull Library
(Godber collection)

By the turn of the century the sparkling stream captured in Brees' sketch of 1843 was fast becoming a drain. Cattle carcases are here being cut into sides at the Ngauranga abattoir.
Alexander Turnbull Library (New Zealand Meat Packers collection)

In 1910 the floor of the gorge had been filled with the meat works, a landmark until the 1970s. In the foreground are the workers' houses, each small lot with its collection of sheds at the back boundary — tool shed, privy, hencoop. Between houses and sheds are the back yards, just large enough to hang out the washing, sit in the sun and try to ignore the sickly sweet smell of the works, to tend a small garden with a few vegetables, or to contain the family dog. A few hens and sheep share the rough ground behind the sheds.
Alexander Turnbull Library (S.C. Smith)

The oil age of the 1920s brought the Ngauranga gorge its landmark service station with its 24-hour service and collection of tall multi-coloured pumps. There was no such thing as a company service station. Consumers could have any brand they wanted — in this case Plume, Shell, Union, Texaco or Big Tree. Castrol and Mobiloil also feature on the hoardings.
Alexander Turnbull Library (Gordon Burt collection)

Down the road towards the city, almost at the Thorndon reclamation, was the Kaiwharawhara wharf. It was originally a landing place for watermen, the only convenient all-tide landing place in the vicinity. Here a lighter discharges explosives about 1909. The cases and barrels were lowered over the side of the overseas vessel in the stream into small sailing lighters. From Kaiwharawhara they were taken to the nearby explosives store.
Wellington Maritime Museum (A.P. Godber)

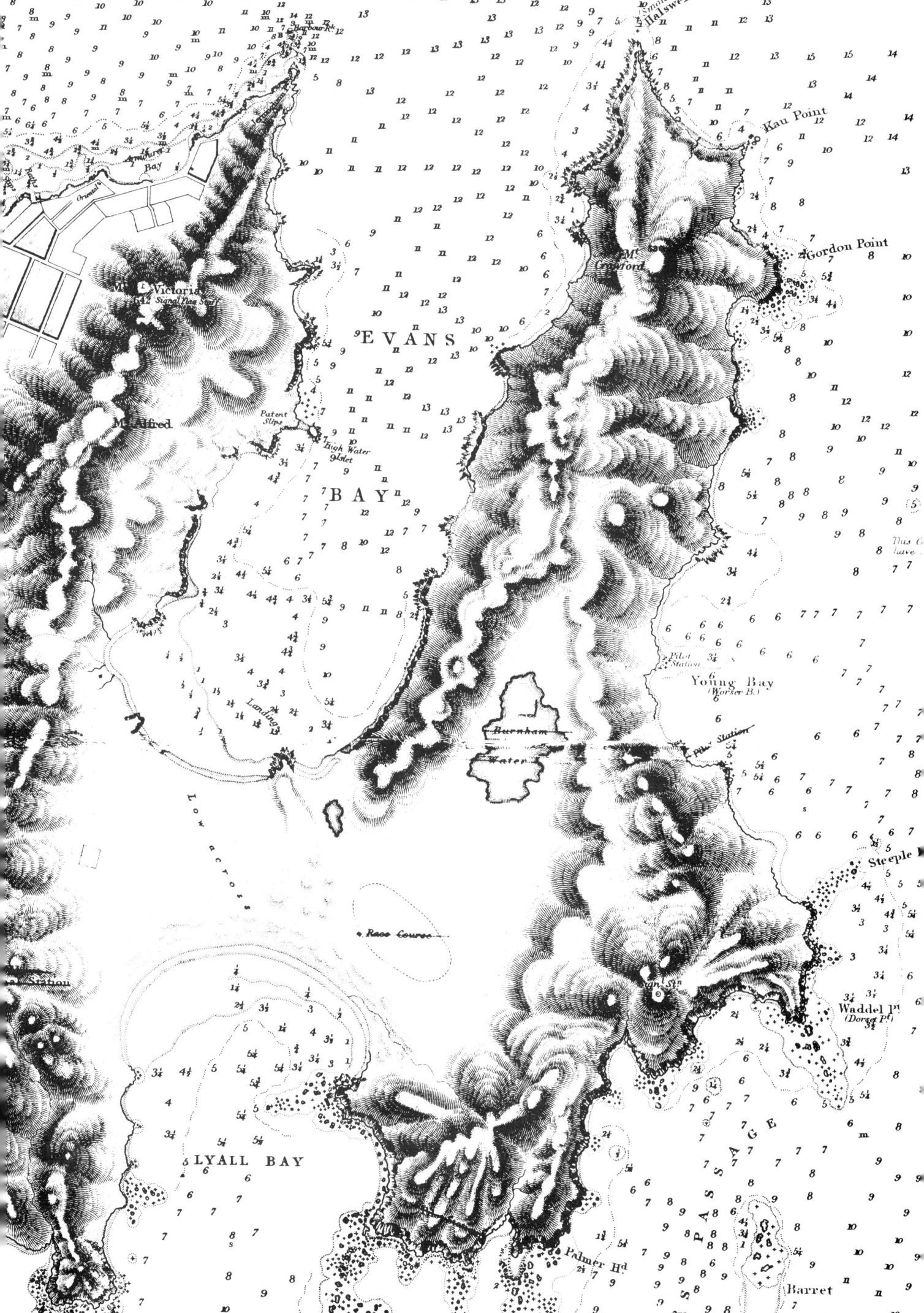

4. Evans Bay and the Miramar Peninsula
From Point Jerningham to Palmer Head

Evans Bay, Lyall Bay, and the Miramar Peninsula, as depicted in Chart BA 1423 (1856).

Tucked into the western side of Evans Bay is Balaena Bay, originally known as Martins Bay. It has always been a place for small boats, and for a couple of decades early this century was the main boat-building and repairing area in Wellington Harbour. Joe Jukes' small shed and slipways attracted many well-known Wellington yachts for their overhauls, and in the years between the two world wars Jukes built many fine fishing vessels as well as yachts. When this photograph was taken, in about 1910, Balaena Bay was just beginning to gain popularity as a site for slipping and overhauls.
Alexander Turnbull Library

By about 1920 activity in Balaena Bay had increased markedly. The yard in the foreground is that of J. Bringans. E.W.P. Bucholz's yacht *Wairere* is on the hard at front left. The steam trawler is having repairs done to her funnel. Around from Bringans' yard is Jukes' slipway.
Alexander Turnbull Library
(S.C. Smith collection)

Evans Bay was for many years a pleasant farming backwater, and a good spot for sailing and fishing. Henry Bates painted the scene in 1857.
Alexander Turnbull Library (Henry Stratton Bates, Evans Bay, near Wellington)

The emptiness of Evans Bay seen from Shelly Bay, looking south-west. About half way along the hills on the far side of the Bay is the site of the Wellington Patent Slip, completed in 1873, the year A.T. Bothamley painted this scene.
Alexander Turnbull Library (Arthur Thomas Bothamley, Evans Bay, Port Nicholson, New Zealand, 26 Dec 1873*)*

The Wellington Patent Slip was a major ship repairing centre until the death of coastal shipping with the introduction of the Cook Strait roll-on-roll-off ferries. The jetty beside the slip and the area just behind the point became the repair and maintenance headquarters for the Union Steam Ship Company. On the other side of the bay there are few signs of habitation.
Alexander Turnbull Library (Dickie collection)

Industry in a rural setting. The steamers *Hawera*, a Patea cheese-and-butter trader, and *Haupiri*, one of the Union Company's fleet, occupy the slipway about 1910.
Alexander Turnbull Library

While the boilermakers and
engineers toil just below, the scene
above them is one of tranquillity as
horses graze at Hataitai.
Alexander Turnbull Library

Between the wars Hataitai grew, as housebuilding spilled over the hills
behind and spread along the bay from developments at the head. In the
Hataitai shopping centre Morey's Pharmacy and the Post and Telegraph
Office shared "The Realm". Walter Stears' shop, on the near side of the
road, was typical of many corrugated iron buildings around the suburbs.
The road is being upgraded and new kerbing is being laid.
Alexander Turnbull Library (Wellington City Council collection)

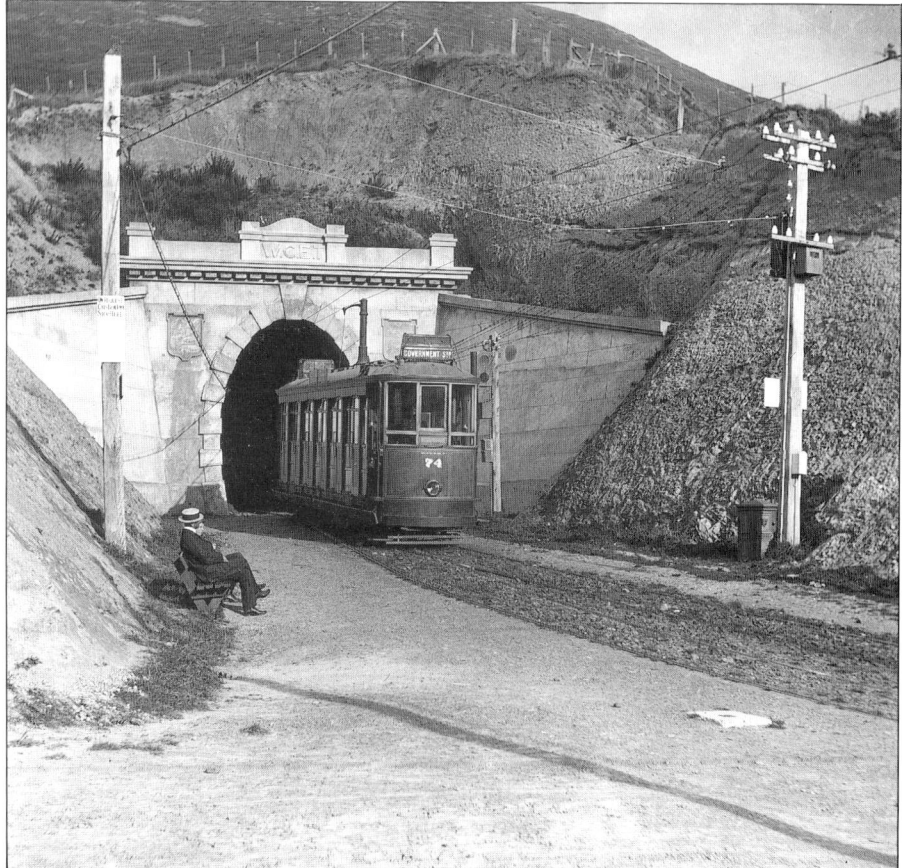

The tramway gave Hataitai and the area at the head of the bay sufficient appeal to lure housing. These men are beginning the excavation of the Hataitai Tunnel from the city end.
Alexander Turnbull Library

A tram emerges from the Hataitai Tunnel.
Alexander Turnbull Library

As housing development, trams, and then motor cars brought more people to Evans Bay, amenities for visitors were provided, such as this bathing shed.
Alexander Turnbull Library

Boatsheds and slipways were built along the shore below Hataitai, and Evans Bay gained its own yachting and boating clubs. It was a great place for a weekend drive to look at the boats, see what was happening at the Patent Slip, and take a bracing walk.
Alexander Turnbull Library
(S.C. Smith collection)

Summer, 1929, and flags are flying from the boatshed. Despite the large number of people, there are no adults in the water. The shingly beach was not a great attraction to swimmers — except for children, who are happy with water wherever it is. Afternoon tea could be bought at the boatshed for sixpence.
Alexander Turnbull Library
(S.C. Smith collection)

At the head of Evans Bay in the 1930s, villas with zig-zag paths linking their front gates to their front doors are perched on the hill. On the flat are rows of houses and the sawtooth roofs of warehouses. At the rear is Rongotai, still largely wasteland.
Alexander Turnbull Library
(S.C. Smith collection)

Separating Evans Bay from the harbour entrance is Miramar Peninsula. It
was known as Watts Peninsula by the early Pakeha settlers, but in 1872
J.C. Crawford, who farmed much of the area, renamed it Miramar, which
is Spanish for Behold the Sea. For many years after the major part of the
peninsula was subdivided for housing the Crawford family retained a
substantial area at its southern end. The original Crawford home,
Miramar, was close to the present golf course. This is the later home. In
the background is the chimney of the Miramar gasworks.
Alexander Turnbull Library (S.C. Smith collection)

The Wellington Golf Club's links were opened on former Crawford land by Lord Glasgow in 1896. It was a cold, blustery day as members gathered at their new clubhouse.
Alexander Turnbull Library (A.P. Ferguson collection)

On a more clement occasion members of the Golf Club pose outside the enlarged clubhouse. Cloth hats and ties were essential parts of a golfer's wardrobe.
Alexander Turnbull Library (A.P. Ferguson collection)

The flats to the south of Miramar
Peninsula were windswept, open,
and wild. It was ideal camping
country for a group requiring
plenty of room to manoeuvre. In
1898 bell tents were pitched for a
military encampment.
Alexander Turnbull Library

Much of Miramar Peninsula was covered in flax in the early days of
Wellington's settlement. The central area of the flat was a lake, with
extensive swamps. Flax was harvested for more than 60 years, the yield
falling as drainage and land development reduced the area of the swamp.
This group of farm employees pauses for lunch in the shelter provided by
hanks of flax hung over a wire fence.
Alexander Turnbull Library (S.C. Smith collection)

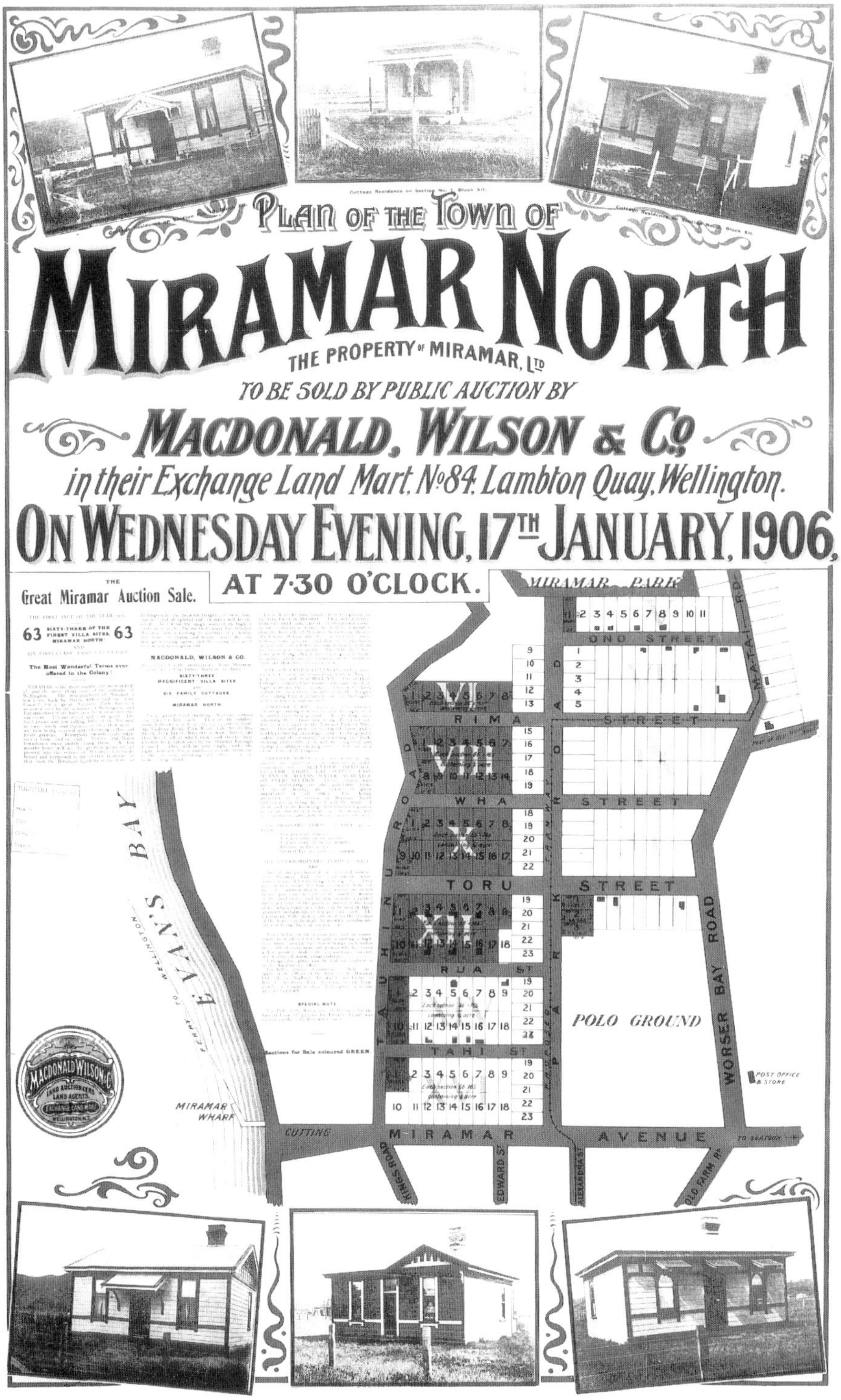

PLAN OF THE TOWN OF

MIRAMAR NORTH

THE PROPERTY of MIRAMAR, LTD

TO BE SOLD BY PUBLIC AUCTION BY

MACDONALD, WILSON & Cº

in their Exchange Land Mart, Nº 84, Lambton Quay, Wellington.

ON WEDNESDAY EVENING, 17TH JANUARY, 1906,

AT 7·30 O'CLOCK.

This 1906 auction of residential sections offered 63 villa sites and six "first-class family cottages". The dark coloured sections shown on the map had been sold previously, and the six cottages illustrated were built on lots in the block bounded by Tauhinu, Wha, Park and Rua roads. The lots offered at this auction were generally those on the western side of Park Road, soon to receive a tramway, and those facing Miramar Park. Those to the east of Park Road were reserved for a later sale. Purchasers at the 1905 auction were said to have made profits of 200 to 300 percent in a year. Terms of purchase were generous: 10 percent down, 10 percent in six months, 10 percent at 12 months and the balance after five years. The interest rate was 5 percent.
Alexander Turnbull Library

The Miramar Wharf was built in 1901, promoted by C.J. and A.D. Crawford who, with other landowners, were anxious to provide access to Wellington for prospective buyers at their land subdivision sales. The Miramar Ferry Company was formed and ran the *Loyalty* and *Admiral* between the city and three wharves on the Miramar Peninsula. From the wharf a deep cut was dug through Rongotai Ridge to allow easy access to the land beyond. Here a group of residents watch the pick-and-shovel gang at work.
Alexander Turnbull Library (S.C. Smith collection)

On the eastern side of Rongotai
Ridge the Wellington Gas
Company built its new works,
moving there from Courtenay Place
in 1907. Into the pleasant green
valley, the "level plains and low
rolling hills" described by the
auctioneer's advertisement in
1906, came this coal-eating,
smoke-belching monster.
*Alexander Turnbull Library
(S.C. Smith collection)*

The Gas Company equipped itself
with modern petrol trucks and the
shipping companies fitted their
vessels with grabs, but down in the
hold there were still grimy,
sweating men shovelling coal from
the sides of the hold into the
centre where the grab could pick it
up.
*Alexander Turnbull Library
(Gordon Burt collection)*

At Miramar North, at the end of the new tramline, the Miramar Athletic
Park and Wonderland Company built its "Mecca of Merry Souls",
Wonderland. Wonderland was designed to rival Days Bay. To get to it was
in itself an outing, and going on an outing was an important aspect of
Edwardian weekend culture. Visitors had the choice of a ferry ride from
the city and a stroll through the cutting past the gasworks, or a ride from
Wellington on a clanging tramcar. Once there, there was all the fun of the
fair: mirrors, clowns, bands, the water chute, Katzenjammer Castle, a
helter-skelter, fireworks, and a Japanese tea house. Here it nears
completion, a magnificent creation almost in the countryside.
Alexander Turnbull Library (S.C. Smith collection)

One of the routes taken by Bell's sightseeing buses was the winding coast
road from the city through Oriental Bay, around Point Jerningham to
Evans Bay and on around the Miramar Peninsula. This bus has paused at
Point Halswell, the northern tip of the peninsula, to allow its passengers
to watch the ships go by. The Union Steam Ship Company's *Maunganui*
leads the smaller twin-funnelled *Tamahine* out of port. The *Tamahine*,
which ran in the Wellington–Picton service for 37 years from 1925, was
reputed to list heavily as soon as she reached the open waters of Cook
Strait from the shelter of Wellington Heads or Tory Channel, maintaining
her list until she reached sheltered waters on the other side.
Alexander Turnbull Library (Just collection)

At Mahanga Bay, north of Point Gordon in the shadow of Mt Crawford, was Fort Dorset. When the naval or military volunteers were in residence for their annual training they usually held an open day for friends and relatives. Sometimes the Steam Ferry Company ran a special service to allow Wellingtonians in general to see how the men in uniform spent their time in camp. On this open day in 1907 the crowd awaits the return of the band while sailors carry trays of teacups up the path in the centre of the photograph. The *Janie Seddon* is berthed at the wharf.
Alexander Turnbull Library (S.C. Smith collection)

The Naval Kazoo Band at the
Mahanga Bay camp, 1908. Their
hatbands proclaim their
membership of the Wellington
Naval Artillery Volunteers (WNAV).
*Alexander Turnbull Library
(S.C. Smith collection)*

When the Karaka Bay wharf was
built by the Seatoun Road Board in
1901, there were few dwellings
nearby.
Norman Wilkinson

Karaka Bay's development edged
along the road southwards,
towards the much larger and older
settlement of Seatoun at the
southern end of Worser Bay.
Northwards is Scorching Bay, and
beyond it Point Gordon.
Auckland Public Library

For a brief period the Wellington
Ferry Company, which ran to Days
Bay, became involved in spirited
competition with the local
Miramar Ferry Company for the
Miramar Peninsula service, but in
1906 the companies merged their
fleets. Here the *Cobar*, which
served from 1906 until 1949,
glides towards Karaka Bay wharf.

South of Karaka Bay is Worser Bay, site of the Wellington pilot station from 1860. The township of Seatoun was subdivided by J.C. Crawford and auctioned in 1878. The sweep of Karaka Bay attracted many Wellington families to build holiday homes there. In 1923 holiday houses and the homes of a sprinkling of permanent residents straggled north from Seatoun township, along the length of the beach. The surf club has turned out for opening day.
Wellington Maritime Museum

On Anniversary day, 22 January 1908, Karaka Bay is crowded for the carnival. The hillsides are almost bare except for a large sign announcing "THE KIOSK".
Auckland Institute and Museum
*(*The Weekly News*)*

Worser Bay Wellington N.Z. 1923

Seatoun is beyond Point Dorset, at the top of the photograph. On the near side of Point Dorset is Breaker Bay, and in the foreground Eve Bay. The ground at and immediately above high water mark was raised by the 1855 earthquake, but the earthquake ridge was destroyed by the building of a coast road. On the point in the centre is a shingle crusher. A solitary boatshed occupies the middle of Eve Bay. The rocks of these bays and those off Flax, Reed and Palmer bays to the south were renowned for their crayfish population.
Alexander Turnbull Library
(Adkin collection)

Palmer Head. To the left, Port Nicholson; to the right, Cook Strait. It must have been a public holiday; the Eastbourne Borough Council's ferries *Duchess* and *Muritai*, with bunting flying, appear to have been out on an excursion. A tanker accompanies them back to harbour. On the ridge of Palmer Head a number of hardy walkers, buttoned up in overcoats, brace themselves against the fresh Cook Strait breeze.
Alexander Turnbull Library
(S.C. Smith collection)

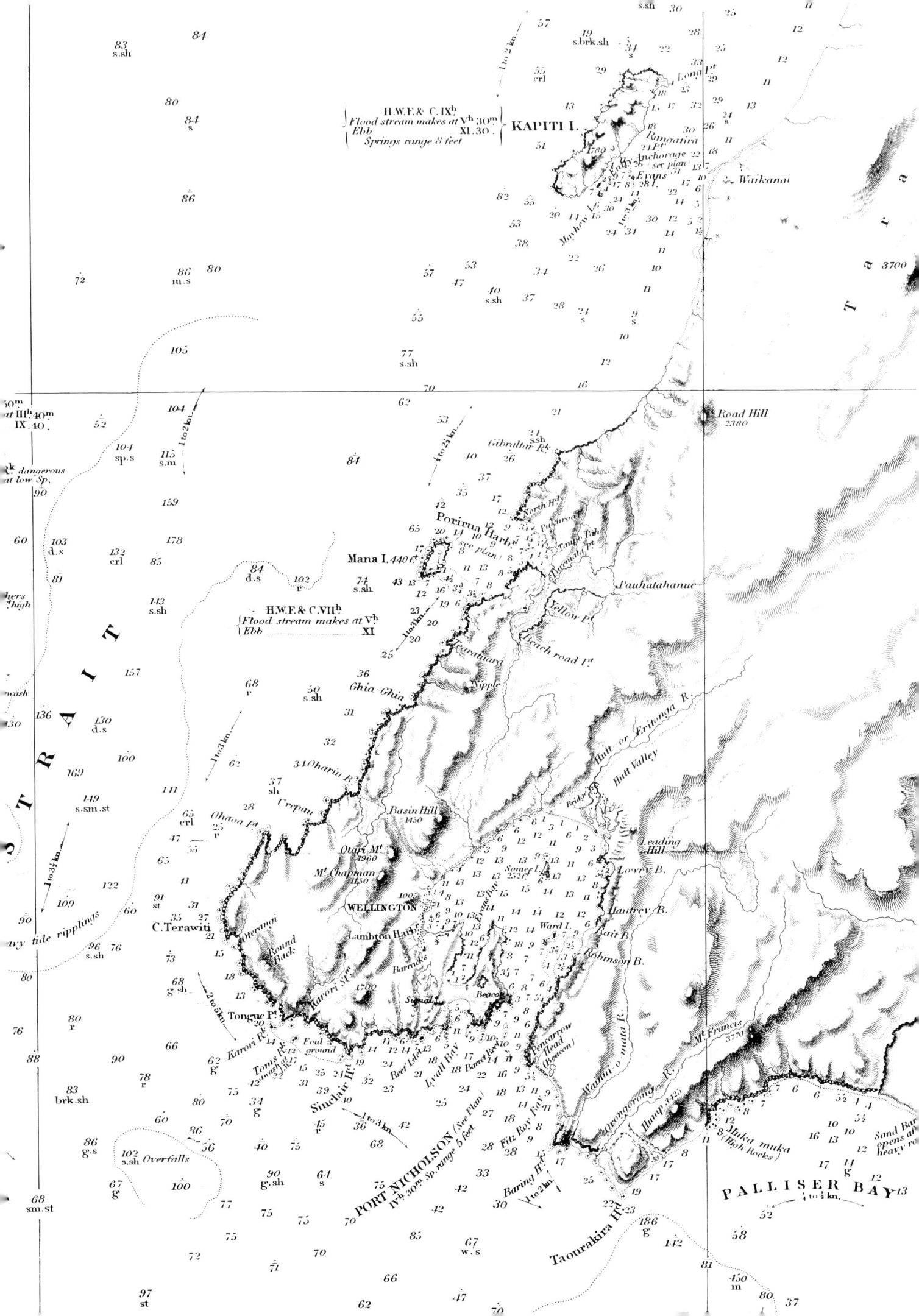

5.   Wild Coast
From Palmer Head to
Makara Beach

Chart BA 2054 (1858) shows the wild coastline of the approaches to the shelter of Port Nicholson.

The coast facing south to Cook Strait is open to the wind and rolling seas. Most of this coast is steep, rocky and inhospitable, but before the steep western hills are reached there are two seaside suburbs: Lyall Bay and Island Bay. Here, at Lyall Bay, two young women and their children enjoy the beach, despite the handicap of their fashionable hats.
Alexander Turnbull Library

The real development of Wellington's southern and south-eastern suburbs came with the trams. In 1909 the first tram reached Lyall Bay.
*Auckland Public Library (*Weekly Graphic and New Zealand Mail*)*

On a calm summer's day the grand sweep of Lyall Bay attracted huge crowds from the city. A few children swam, but most visitors promenaded, gossiped, and visited the tea rooms.
Alexander Turnbull Library (Field collection)

At the height of the summer season tents were pitched, and the lifesaving and surf clubs flew their flags. The large building on the left is a tea room. Outside is a crowded double-decker tram. By 1910 crinolines were no longer obligatory, and most of the young ladies are showing their ankles. Gentlemen all wear hats, but a few are bold enough to be seen at the beach without a tie.
Alexander Turnbull Library

By the early thirties pudding-basin hats were the height of fashion for women. The man in the foreground, although clothed ready for a swim, wears a woolly tam-o'-shanter. Even on a fine day the Cook Strait breeze could keep Lyall Bay's visitors well wrapped up.
Alexander Turnbull Library

Cars took over from trams. Here the Parade at Lyall Bay is tarsealed in front of the Grand View Tea Room — "The best in the Bay" according to the sign on the roof. The tea room sold Big Tree motor spirit and specialised in catering for motor parties. The house past the tea room was the home of the local taxi proprietor.
Alexander Turnbull Library
(S.C. Smith collection)

Sometimes Lyall Bay could offer unusual attractions. Here a crowd gathers to inspect the carcase of a beached whale while small boys stand on top of it. It must have been recently beached. A few days later even the fresh air of Cook Strait would be insufficient to blow away the stench.
Alexander Turnbull Library
(S.C. Smith collection)

On an unusually calm day in 1934 this Cant 25 floatplane from the Italian cruiser *Armando Diaz* paid Lyall Bay a visit.
Alexander Turnbull Library (Evening Post)

In 1939 Lyall Bay became the site of the New Zealand Centennial Exhibition. Here the impressive exhibition buildings occupy a large part of the bay frontage. Many visitors came to Wellington expressly to see the exhibition and stayed at a motor camp set up nearby to accommodate them. The Eastbourne ferries ran special trips to Miramar Wharf in the weekends. The exhibition looked forward rather than back, seeking to confirm New Zealand's nationhood. The celebrations lost their sheen as the dark shadow of the Second World War fell.
Alexander Turnbull Library (Hall-Raine collection)

Beauty and the boats. A fashionably dressed young lady poses for the photographer. Island Bay's first settlers fished the waters of Cook Strait in small sailing dinghies such as these. In the stern of the boat farthest from the camera is a wicker crayfish pot. In the background is Taputeranga Island, which gives the bay its name.
Alexander Turnbull Library (Henry Wright collection)

The 1884 Volunteers' Easter camp at Island Bay drew a big crowd on its open day. Visitors throng the hill (left rear) and the ridge in the foreground as the artillery creates noise and smoke and the cavalry dash across the flat land to the left.
Alexander Turnbull Library
(G.E. Pearce collection)

This military gathering was not such a light-hearted affair. The Second Contingent of the New Zealand Expeditionary Force is reviewed at Island Bay on 18 January 1900 before sailing to fight the Boers in South Africa.
Alexander Turnbull Library

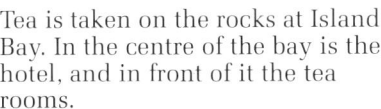

Tea is taken on the rocks at Island Bay. In the centre of the bay is the hotel, and in front of it the tea rooms.
Alexander Turnbull Library
(H.G. Tonks collection)

In 1909 Island Bay was rapidly changing from a small Italian fishing community to another dormitory suburb. Neat rows of new houses face newly formed streets. Paling fences protect new gardens from the Cook Strait breeze. On the extreme left is C. & A. Odlin's timber yard, well positioned in a thriving new suburb. The sign on the store opposite extols the virtues of Nelson Moate's teas — purity, quality, value and strength — while a tram rumbles towards Wellington.
Alexander Turnbull Library
(S.C. Smith collection)

The foreshore was a boat repair yard, a storage place for things nautical, a net drying area, and a lobster-pot factory. This fisherman works on his boat.
Alexander Turnbull Library
(L.J. Paul collection)

By 1920 the tiny sailing dinghies were making way for motor launches, but the foreshore was still the boatyard. The closer the boat to the door of the fisherman's house the better.
Alexander Turnbull Library
(R.M. Mack collection)

Island Bay didn't attract as many beach devotees as Lyall Bay, but it had its followers. The building on the far right is the ladies' bathing shed. The men's bathing shed was well away, in a separate building in the centre.
Alexander Turnbull Library (S.C. Smith collection)

Speeches open the season at the Island Bay Surf Lifesaving Club, 1926.
Alexander Turnbull Library (S.C. Smith collection)

The speeches are over, and club members demonstrate their skills. On the left is the diving stage.
Alexander Turnbull Library (S.C. Smith collection)

The diving stage at Island Bay was the training platform for many a fine diver. While his elders show what they can do the small boy in the foreground is using an empty biscuit tin as a flotation aid.
Alexander Turnbull Library (R.W. Archer collection)

The Island Bay fishermen were a sporting crowd. This is their 1921 rugby team.
Alexander Turnbull Library (S.C. Smith collection)

For all their sea-lore, the fishermen of Island Bay sometimes fell victim to the gales and huge seas that frequently swept their coast. In September 1933 a group of Island Bay boats headed for home when the weather deteriorated. One, the *Santina*, had engine problems. She was overwhelmed by the gale, her four crewmen were drowned, and her wreckage was strewn along the shore. Here Island Bay fishermen set out to hold the funeral service at sea.
Alexander Turnbull Library (S.C. Smith collection)

West from Island Bay are The
Sirens Rocks, then Owhiro Bay at
the mouth of Happy Valley. It's a
small, isolated bay, but an ideal
spot to boil a billy.
Alexander Turnbull Library
(Henry Wright collection)

Despite its exposure to the weather
Owhiro Bay had a handful of
houses. From the back of the bay
the road climbs up the valley to
Brooklyn. The bay also had an
industry; it supplied beach gravel
to Wellington's building trade.
Alexander Turnbull Library
(M. Johnson collection)

Tonks and Andrews collected beach stones and shingle the hard way, shovelling it onto a dray. From the beach it was taken up a ramp on the landward side of the road and tipped onto a stockpile for screening.
Alexander Turnbull Library (S.C. Smith collection)

From Tonks and Andrews' stockpile the gravel was trucked up the valley and over the hill. The trucks that ran the route were known as the Happy Valley gravel runabouts.
Alexander Turnbull Library (S.C. Smith collection)

▷ Further around the coast at Makara Beach was another fishing community. Unlike that at Island Bay, this community attracted few visitors. Apart from being something of a curiosity piece for those town dwellers that made the effort to walk to the beach, it was self sufficient. It was proud, perhaps even opinionated about its character. These Makara Beach fishermen strike a pose.
Alexander Turnbull Library (J.N. Taylor collection)

In May 1931 the coastal steamer *Progress* broke her tailshaft, lost her propeller, and resorted to sails. Little by little, over a period of half a day, she was dragged slowly towards the rocks until eventually she hit, was lifted off, hit again, and was smashed. Frantic rescue efforts by policemen and others resulted in eight crew members being saved, but four drowned. Here, in the early afternoon of 1 May 1931, the *Progress* (the lumpy shape, top right) her back broken, is pounded to pieces off Owhiro Bay.
Alexander Turnbull Library (S.C. Smith collection)

On special occasions the fishermen of Makara dressed in their best. On New Year's Day 1905 they flew their bunting as visitors walked down their main street.
Alexander Turnbull Library (Hislop collection)

These fishermen are doing what fishermen do when they aren't fishing. They potter about with their boats, they yarn, and they talk to the dog. The Makara fishermen's boats were small, but they were good, strong, clinker-built dinghies, suitable for fishing in and around the rocks and solid enough to take the pounding of the seas and being hauled up the stony beach.
Alexander Turnbull Library (Hislop collection)

Leopold Haupois was a Makara fisherman. He was reputed to have
arrived in New Zealand in 1875 from his native Normandy. After felling
timber in the Hutt and working on farms he drifted to Makara where,
known as French Louis, he fished and lived in the tiny community until
his death at the age of 87. It was said that Lady Bledisloe, whose husband
was Governor-General from 1930 to 1935, used to have conversations
with French Louis to practice her French.
Alexander Turnbull Library

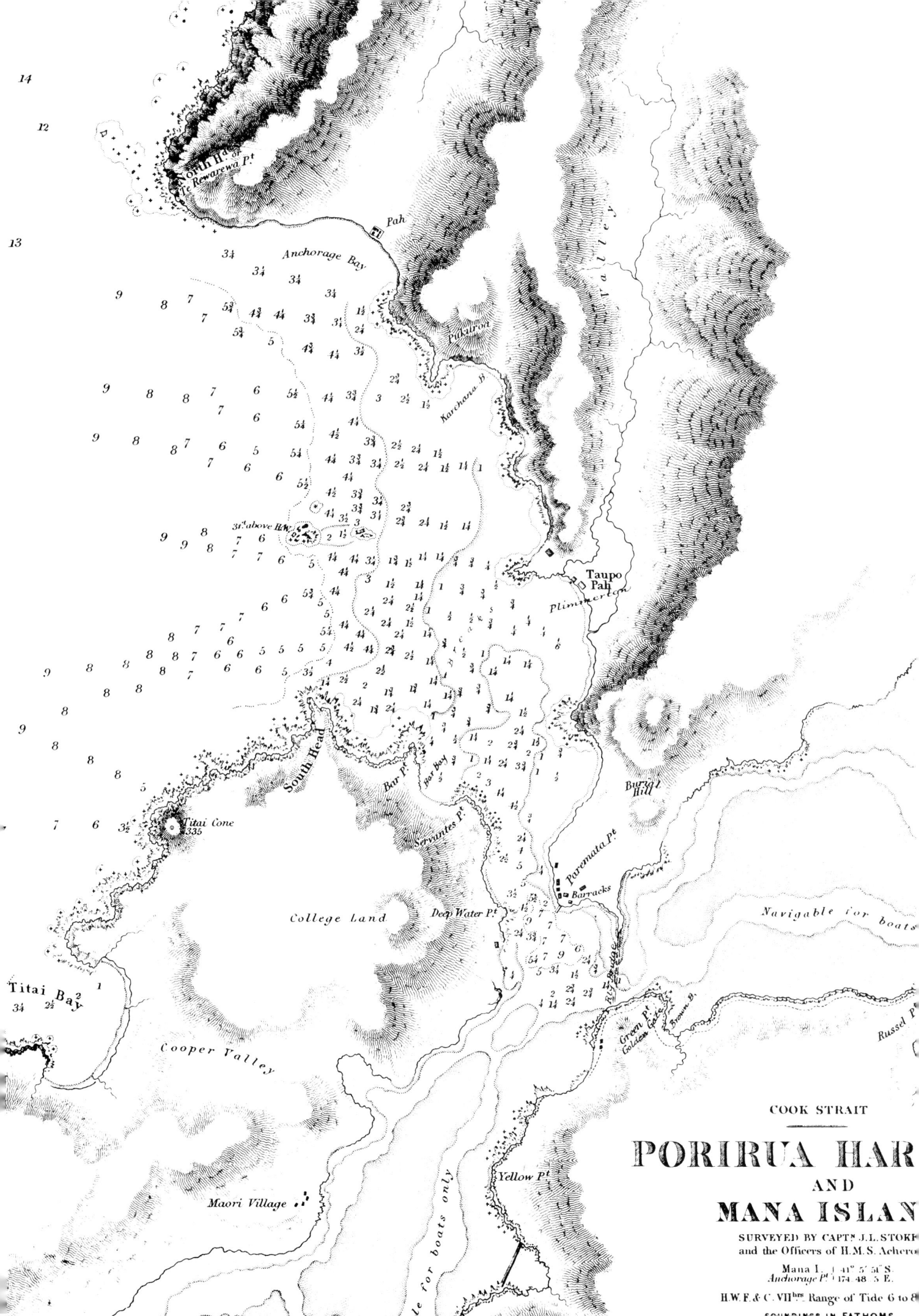

14

12

13

North Id. or
Te Rewarewa Pt.

Pah

34   Anchorage Bay
    3¼   3¼
9   8   7 5¾ 4¾ 4¼ 3¼   3¼   3¾
        7   5¼   4¾ 4¼   3¼   2¼

                    Pukatroa

9   8   8   7   6   5½ 4¼ 3¾ 3   2½ 1½
        7   6   5¼ 4¼   Karehana B.
9   8   8 7   6   5   4½   3¾ 2½ 2¼ 1½ 1¼
        7   6   5¼   4¼ 3¾ 2½ 2¼ 1½ 1¼ 1
                     5½   4¼

9   9   8   3ft above H.W. 4¼ 3¾ 2¾ 2½ 1½ 1¼
        8   3ft above H.W. 7 6   4¼ 3¾ 3¼ 2¾ 2¼ 1½ 1¼
               7 6   2 1½   3 2¾ 2¼ 1½ 1¼
                                              Taupo
9   9   8   7   6   4¼ 4¼ 3¼ 1½ 1½ 1¼ 1½   Pah
        8   7   6   4¼ 1½ 1¼ ¼   Plimmerton
            7   6   5   5½ 4¼   3 ¾
                5¼ 4¼   2½ 2½ 1 ¾
        8   7   7   6   5 4½ 4¼   ¾
        8   8   8 6   5 5 5 5½ 4¼ 4¼ 2¼ 1½ 1¼ ¾ ½
    9   8   8   8 7   6   5   5 4 2¼ 2¼ 1¾ 1¼ ¾ ¾
        8   8   7   6   5   2¼ 2¼ 1¾ ¾ 1¼
9   8   8   7   6   1¾ ¾
        8   5¼ 4¼ 2½ 2½ 1 ¾ 1½
    8   2½ 1¾ 1¼ ¾
9   8   8   South Head   1¼ 1 Burial
    8   Bar Pt. Hat Bay   Hill
            5   1¾ 2¼ 3¼
7   6   3½   Titai Cone   Servantes Pt. 2¼
            335   2¼
                                    5   Paremata Pt.
                                        Barracks
            College Land   Deep Water Pt.   Navigable for boats
                                   2¼ 3¾ 7 7
                                   5¼ 3½ 7 9 6
Titai Bay   2¼
3¼ 2½   4 2¼ 2¼
                                        4 1¾ 2¼
        Cooper Valley   Green P.   Russel
                                   Golden Gate Brown B.

                    COOK STRAIT

                    PORIRUA HAR

                        AND

                    MANA ISLAN

        Maori Village   Yellow Pt.
                le for boats only

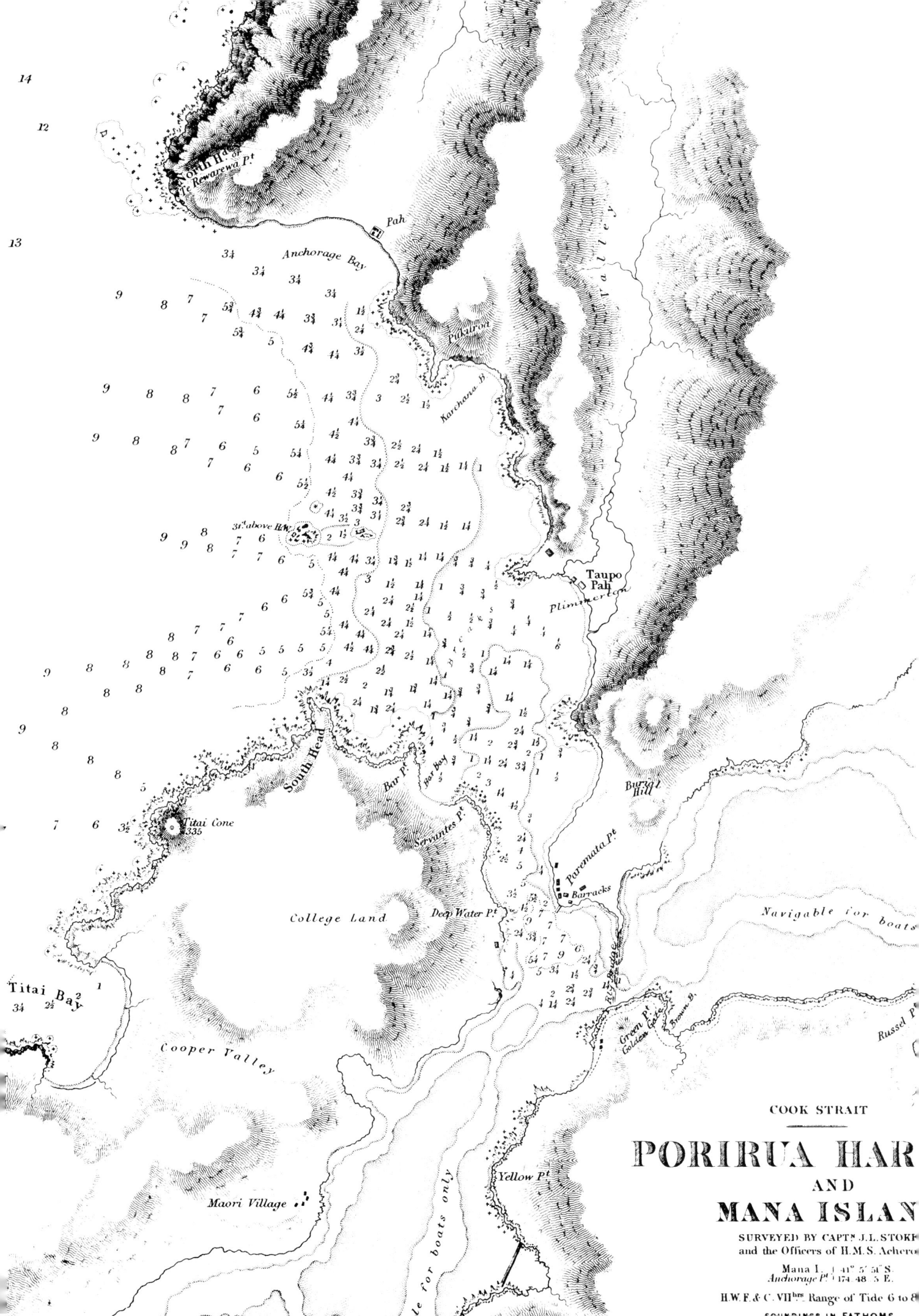

SURVEYED BY CAPTN. J.L. STOKE
and the Officers of H.M.S. Achero

        Mana I. 41° 5′ 51″ S
    Anchorage Pt. 174. 48. 5 E.

H.W. F. & C. VIIhrs. Range of Tide 6 to 8
        SOUNDINGS IN FATHOMS

6. Facing the Tasman Sea
From Titahi Bay and Porirua North to Waikanae

Porirua Harbour as it appeared in the 1858 chart BA 2588.

In the 1920s Titahi Bay was a great sweep of sand surrounded by wilderness. Here and there were holiday cottages, but civilisation was over the hill. This was a coast of long, lonely beaches until the motor car became affordable to many families in the decade after the end of the First World War. By the late twenties Titahi Bay, while preserving its feeling of wide open spaces and near empty hills, was attracting huge numbers of visitors on summer weekends and public holidays. There was plenty of parking space, and the sand was hard enough and smooth enough for drivers to motor along the beach. When there were fewer people about, the beach attracted daring young men who raced their cars at low tide.
Alexander Turnbull Library (G.N.T. Gouldie collection)

When the crowds went home and
the sun began to slide towards the
horizon there was plenty of space
for a young lady and her spaniel.
At the far end of Titahi Bay are
boatsheds and, above them, the
beginnings of housing
development. The large building
towards the left is the tea rooms.
Alexander Turnbull Library
(S.P. Andrew)

A higgledy-piggledy assortment of
bathing sheds to the right of the
track down to the beach, the Titahi
Bay Club to the left. The group of
people on the right near the water
seem to be crowded around some
object of interest, presumably
washed up from the sea.
Alexander Turnbull Library

The Titahi Bay Club was a popular destination for lunch and also provided board for those who wanted a longer stay at the beach. The track in the foreground led to the beach, off to the left. The sign warns drivers of the 15 miles per hour speed limit.
Alexander Turnbull Library (S.C. Smith collection)

Plimmerton in the 1880s was farmland. In the background are Paremata and the entrance to Porirua Harbour.
*Alexander Turnbull Library
(E.R. Williams collection)*

By the mid 1890s Plimmerton was a thriving settlement. The large building on the left is Plimmerton House. To the right of centre a group of men and women are holding hands in a circle. Are they about to perform a dance, or are they about to embark on the favourite picnic game of kiss-in-the-ring?
Alexander Turnbull Library (Wilson collection)

Although there was settlement at the centre of Plimmerton beach, there was plenty of room for a camper to get away from it all in 1909.
Alexander Turnbull Library (S.C. Smith collection)

Karehana Bay. The clinker dinghy
Arahini is dragged to shore, her
sailing done for the day.
*Alexander Turnbull Library
(J.M. Daley collection)*

Converting the old coastal road — in places not much better than a track
— to a coastal highway was a mammoth task which provided
employment for a great many men in the mid 1930s. The
Governor-General, Lord Galway, inspects progress in December 1937
where the new highway descends from Pukerua Bay to the coast. Holiday
cottages can be seen at the beach on the left.
Alexander Turnbull Library (Evening Post collection)

Paekakariki, 26 December 1906. Paekakariki was a railway town, a
huddle of railway houses hard against the lines where spare carriages and
freight cars await their steam locomotives. The road from Wellington
skirts the bottom of the cliff, passing behind the stockpiles of coal at left.
On the right is the pub.
Alexander Turnbull Library (Watt collection)

The men who worked on the stretch of highway between Plimmerton and
Paekakariki lived here in the Pukerua Bay camp. The central amenities
building is under construction at left.
*Alexander Turnbull Library (*Evening Post *collection)*

By 1939 the coastal highway was nearing completion. This section requires a seawall for which foundations are being dug. The site is protected from the tides by a wall of sandbags and a pump is in use. The Centennial Highway was a project to mark New Zealand's centennial in 1940.
Alexander Turnbull Library (Beattie collection)

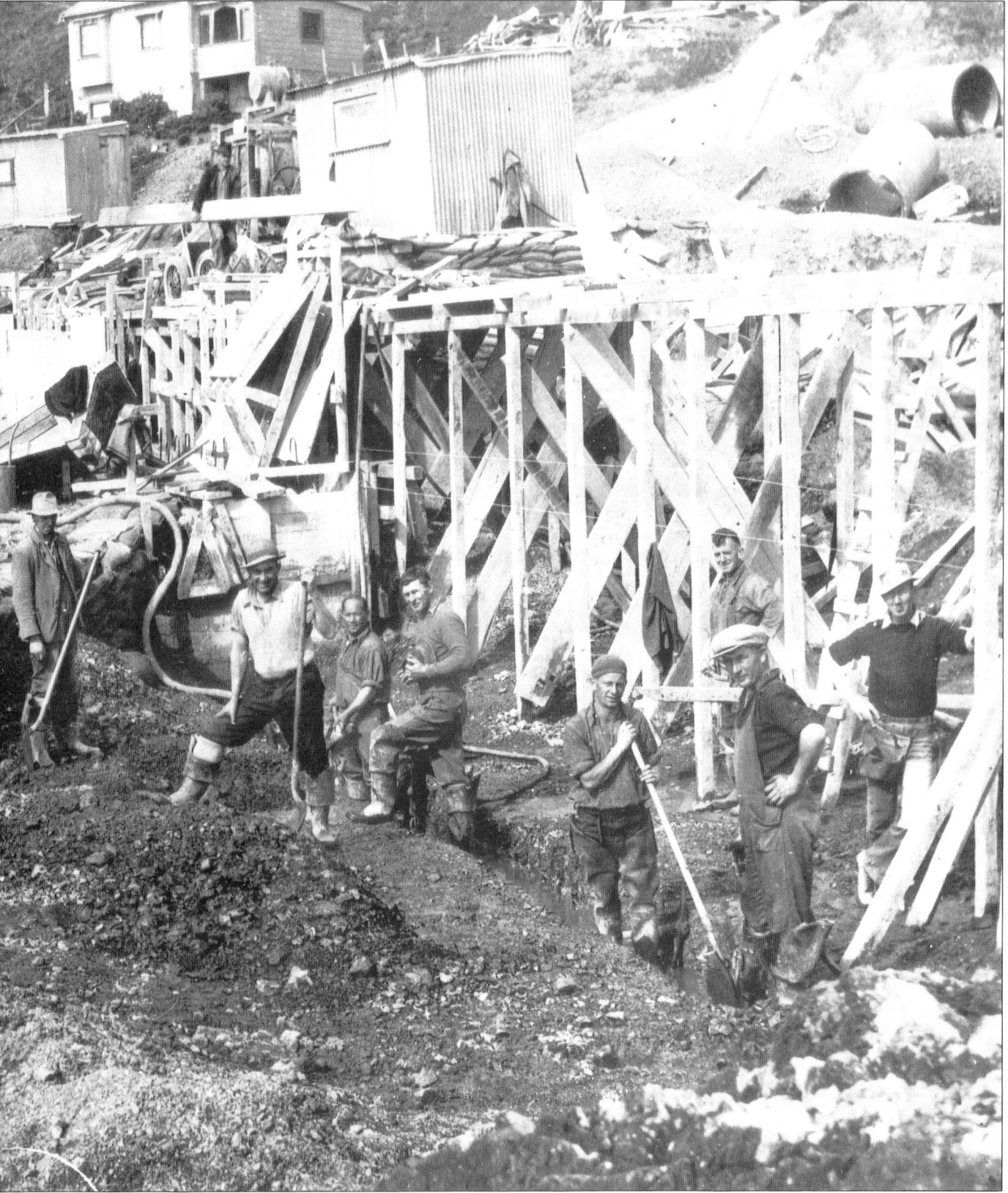

The clubhouse of the Paekakariki Life Saving and Surf Club was the centre of activity on fine summer days. On this occasion in the mid 1920s the crowd waits for the lifesavers to go through their drill. Parasols and a few ordinary umbrellas are raised to ward off the sun.
Alexander Turnbull Library
(S.C. Smith collection)

Those who did not have ringside seats at the clubhouse sat in the sandhills, while others promenaded on the beach.
Alexander Turnbull Library
(E. Lynch collection)

Paraparaumu Beach, 1914. This tent is pitched on what was to be the site of the Majestic Hotel. Over the top of the sandhill is the sea.
Alexander Turnbull Library
(G.H. Howell collection)

The tent was occupied by the Vaughan family. Edna, Arthur and Sebley Vaughan, their sunhats firmly fixed, walk along the track through the sandhills to the beach. *Alexander Turnbull Library (G.H. Howell collection)*

Paraparaumu Beach, 6 January 1938. Midsummer, but not a soul in the water. The crowd has gathered to watch the men in the front row who are attempting to shoot a large shark that has been cruising close to shore. Kapiti Island, once the fortress of Te Rauparaha, is in the background. *Alexander Turnbull Library (C.J. Tustin, from R.J. Meyer collection)*

The main street at Paraparaumu Beach was a battleground for ice cream brands. The Post Office Store at the left advertises Tip-Top, Barker's Tea Rooms in the centre sells Frosty Jack — "The Hygenic Food", while Vincents Milk Bar proclaims Arctic ice cream to be "Delicious and Nutritious". Between the Post Office and Barker's is the general store.
Alexander Turnbull Library (S.C. Smith collection)

There was industry up the coast. At Paraparaumu this tin shed housed Andrew Jack's brass foundry. The truck in front was brand new, the pride and joy of the County Council.
Alexander Turnbull Library (G.H. Howell collection)

In Beach Road, Paraparaumu, this
camp was built to house relief
workers in 1934.
Auckland Public Library

Waikanae in 1905 was a place of
sand and sea. To get to the sea
meant crossing the barrier of the
sandhills. The man in the centre is
a tiny figure amongst the rolling
dunes.
Alexander Turnbull Library

The Whiting and Vaughan encampment at Kapiti, 1920. While the men
pitch tents and set up camp the women establish their kitchen on the beach.
Alexander Turnbull Library (G.H. Howell collection)

The Waikanae River mouth was the departure point for Kapiti Island.
Michael Donovan prepares to take a camping party to Kapiti in his clinker
fishing boat in 1920.
Alexander Turnbull Library (G.H. Howell collection)

Wellington's sightseeing tours pushed further afield in the 1930s. Bell's
Buses join the crowd at Waikanae Beach.
Alexander Turnbull Library (Just collection)

This family is at the Raft Hole on the Waikanae River.
Alexander Turnbull Library

Index